You Gotta Love 'Em

What I've discovered from working
with addiction at Arizona Pathways
Residential Treatment Center

Ellen Gardner, L.I.S.A.C.
Director, Arizona Pathways
"A Holistic Solution to Addictions"

abbott press®
A DIVISION OF WRITER'S DIGEST

You Gotta Love 'Em
What I've Discovered from Working with Addiction at
Arizona Pathways Residential Treatment Center

Copyright © 2012 by Rev. Ellen Gardner, L.I.S.A.C.

ISBN: 978-1-4582-0576-6 (sc)
ISBN: 978-1-4582-0577-3 (e)
ISBN: 978-1-4582-0578-0 (hc)

Library of Congress Control Number: 2012915220

Abbott Press books may be ordered through booksellers or by contacting:

Abbott Press
1663 Liberty Drive
Bloomington, IN 47403
www.abbottpress.com
Phone: 1-866-697-5310

Printed in the United States of America

Abbott Press rev. date: 10/16/12

By Ellen Gardner, L.I.S.A.C.

Director of Arizona Pathways

"A Holistic Solution to Addictions"

Residential and Outpatient Programs

Contents

Dedication

To all individuals experiencing addiction or destructive lifestyles and to those who love them.

I want to express my gratitude to all my teammates who helped bring this book to fruition. Thanks to:

Marie Jones for all the computer work, shared ideas, organization skills, encouragement and friendship.

Mary L. Holden, my friend and editor who so skillfully shaped the manuscript into its final form.

Each and every client of Arizona Pathways of Life, Unity and Love and their families who have been master teachers in the world of substance abuse and addiction.

A special thank you to my husband, Dan, who has stood by my side through all the years, even though he didn't understand what I was doing or why I was doing it.

All of the author's proceeds from the sale of this book will go to Arizona Pathways of Life, Unity and Love to support the expansion and continuing work of providing pathways to freedom from the bondage of addictions.

For more information, or to make a tax-deductible contribution, please visit www.arizonapathways.com.

Foreword:

"...never throw out anyone."

AUDREY HEPBURN SAID, "PEOPLE, EVEN more than things, have to be restored, renewed, revived, reclaimed and redeemed; never throw out anyone." This book is based on the belief that there are no throwaway people. What I say is that *you gotta love 'em.*

Summing up a career in the drug and alcohol rehabilitation field is like spreading out a net to catch dandelion seeds in a strong wind. It took me over 10 years to write this book, but caught in its net are the seeds of my experiences and those of clients. Some names of clients at Arizona Pathways in this book have been changed. May this book help readers who need insights about overcoming their own addictions or learning how to stop the damaging habits of people they love.

One of my favorite legends comes from the Cherokee people. It is the one about the grandfather teaching a grandson about life through the metaphor of wolves. The elder describes two wolves fighting inside his, and everyone's, spirit—the wolf of ego, pride, resentment, anger, superiority, greed; the other wolf of peace, joy, hope, generosity, compassion and love. The grandson asks which wolf will win the fight and the elder answers that the one who "gets fed" will be the survivor.

This story is about the inner conflict that all people experience. The fact that there are two wolves shows the duality with which we all live—peace and trouble. The 'peace wolf' is symbolic of the truth of who and what we are: the perfect expression of our Creator. The 'trouble wolf' is symbolic of the self-identity we create—our ego. This identity expresses our doubts, fears and other qualities we accept as ourselves, our personalities.

Without clear awareness and understanding of these two entities that compose the human personality, people feed *both* wolves. This makes it very difficult to find freedom from struggle. Everything people think, feel and believe is food that feeds both wolves.

The food for the 'peace wolf' contains love, truth, kindness, intelligence, creativity, strength and courage. It is impossible for the 'peace wolf' to consume the foods of the 'trouble wolf.' The 'trouble wolf' has a diet of fear, anger, revenge, helplessness, hopelessness, cowardice, dishonesty, judgment, condemnation, guilt, shame and illness. Sometimes a 'trouble wolf' comes across and eats foods meant for the 'peace wolf' but it prefers the foods meant for trouble. The following is a list of 'wolf food' that shows the contrast between the peace and the trouble:

Thought Food for The Peace Wolf	Thought Food for The Trouble Wolf
I am a child of God.	*I am an addict/alcoholic.*
I am kind and compassionate.	*I must look out for number one.*
All my needs are met easily.	*I work hard and get nowhere.*
I forgive myself. I forgive others.	*I'll get even!*
I know all that happens is for the good.	*Everything goes wrong for me.*
God loves me.	*Nobody loves me.*

I am able to receive love.	*I cannot allow love in.*
I embrace change.	*It's too late to change.*
I take responsibility.	*It's not my fault.*
Life is fun.	*Life is difficult.*
I am happy and healthy.	*I am angry and sick.*
I live in financial ease.	*I'm a loser.*
I gain strength through challenge.	*I can't do anything.*
I am one with all that is life.	*I am all alone.*
Life is change; change is good.	*It's always been terrible.*
Life is an adventure.	*Life is scary.*
All things are possible.	*I cannot escape pain.*

It is easy to see how both wolves get fed without being consciously aware. Feeding both wolves provides them with endurance to continue to see, feel and experience struggle—especially the struggle to face the limiting effects of addiction. When you become conscious of the wolf you are feeding, you also become conscious of the wolves you help others to feed. Take care to carry only food that will feed the 'peace wolf' in your own heart and in the hearts of other people.

Humanity must learn to live with the duality of peace and trouble. The two wolves will always be with us. It only takes awareness to see what is happening with hunger and fulfillment. When the 'trouble wolf' eats the foods of the 'peace wolf' a shift occurs. Be aware of the inner wolf being fed in order to feel the shift. After awhile, the right diet of 'wolf food' will make itself known as you learn to feed both wolves the food of peace. As this new pattern of feeding comes into view, faith builds.

At the foundation of rehabilitation is faith. Even just a small amount may be all it takes to get someone's life going in a better direction. As Jesus said to his disciples, "For truly I say to you, if there is faith in you even as a grain of mustard seed, you will say to this mountain, 'move away from here' and it will move away, and nothing will prevail over you." (Matt.17:20). Regardless of your religious orientation or your concept of spirituality, faith is one of the strongest tools for healing human beings. You can't see it, but when it is there, you can feel it with your heart.

Chapter 1:

The Evolution of Addiction Treatment

WE SEEM TO BE STUCK in the ways we treat addiction in our society. Any treatment is better than no treatment, but there has been an evolution in how addictions are understood and treated. This book represents the next step in that evolution.

Town drunk, disease and finally...a new way

In terms of evolution, this book can begin with the story of the town drunk. Most towns had at least one town drunk; big cities had lots of town drunks. The traditional way of treating them was to accept these people in their role as the town drunk, to protect them from themselves and to try to help their families by providing food and shelter. My grandfather was a town drunk so my mother and her siblings grew up on welfare. They grew up with the shame of their father's role as the town drunk as various friends and neighbors gave them handouts. That was common.

Another example of the town drunk is the character of Otis on the "Andy Griffith Show," a popular TV show in the 1960s and in reruns. A drunk Otis was picked up by the sheriff, brought to jail, slept it off, had a meal and then went back on his way. Sometimes he arrived at the jail and locked himself in until he became sober. That is how substance abuse used to be dealt with on TV.

The next phase of evolution was when E.M. Jelnik, the "Father of Alcohol Studies" shifted people's awareness from the "sin" of drunkenness to the concept of alcoholism as "disease." This was an improvement because people who are sick get sympathy and treatment.

Alcoholics were finally seen as people who did not choose to get sick, so they became deserving of getting help to become cured. The town drunk became a patient. Society acknowledged that the town drunk could not be held responsible for handling what life gave him or her. They were no longer judged or criticized. The drunks became victims and sufferers of a disease called addiction.

Opinion polls now find that over 80 percent of those who respond say that addiction is an illness. The National Council on Alcoholism, the American Medical Association, the American Hospital Association and Alcoholics Anonymous have all put efforts into lobbying, public education and publications to promote this point of view.

Formulation of alcoholism as a disease opened up possibilities for treatment that were never before available. And now, we have a disease that is not only incurable, but is an epidemic. It is carried from generation to generation by the belief in the power of disease and a genetic predisposition to it.

It is time for the next step. In this book I propose that addiction be seen as a natural tendency. Not as a disease, but a propensity. As human beings, we all seek relief. We all want to feel joy. The addict seeks joy and relief in substances that destroy bodies. When given a chance—in an environment that does not judge or punish, but instead exposes them to the deep nature of who they are—to find relief for their suffering, they may heal.

Because of the overwhelming number of people who are struggling with addictions and because of the tremendous pain this brings to the people who love them, I have sought understanding and wisdom in order to respond to the need. This book allows me to share what I've discovered at the treatment center I founded: Arizona Pathways. My point of view is non-traditional. It is the result of prayer, meditation, personal experience, shared experiences, the reading of volumes of books and other publications and attending many seminars.

I have come to believe that while addiction is destructive, it is also natural. Working on the essence of ourselves, our spirits, teaches that even if the human tendency is to fight or flee an enemy, fear, disappointment, grief or despair, healing can only come after the enemies are faced and embraced. Addiction is to be embraced, not fought.

The reason we are losing the war on drugs is because we are fighting a natural human tendency. Drugs are not attacking us. Drugs are not the enemy. Humanity is the enemy. It is time to view addiction with the spiritual insight that many of us have been gaining through our work in addiction.

We are ready to go to the next step.

What would happen if everyone looked at themselves and everyone else around them as God's spiritual offspring, as expressions of one creative source? What if we eliminated all the labels such as addict, gifted, handicapped, convict, saint, sinner, or even red, yellow, black, white, pretty, plain, fat, thin, bipolar, schizophrenic, ADD, smart, stupid? It seems that people do become the person they are labeled to be and then they accept the limitations of those labels.

Whether it is a label given to others or one we accept as our own, freedom comes only when we are true to ourselves—when we stop seeing and believing in the labels. Saying this and living the concept of being true to one's self is quite different.

Millions of people choose to live as addicts and alcoholics: as victims of society, race, gender, adverse childhood experiences or other injuries. Many of us identify as some or all of the above. Of course, we have positive roles we play: parent, teacher, son, daughter, wife, husband, employee, employer, singer, artist, healer. Of all the things we do and are, we are created from one source, God or a Supreme Being or a Unity Consciousness— whatever you choose to call it—and by accepting that we are greater than the restrictions of our bodies, we get free of the limitations given by roles, labels and in having a false idea of the true self.

The path to Arizona Pathways

Life is difficult.

Creating change to make things better in life can be even more difficult.

I have studied books, accumulated work experience, passed the exam and paid the fees to become a licensed independent substance abuse counselor (L.I.S.A.C.). At an entirely different level, my understanding of addictive behavior comes from the experiences I share with my clients. We approach substance abuse as a team, working through trial and error to find a solution.

Our work is more discovery than recovery, more healing than treatment.

It is an ongoing adventure that is challenging, frustrating, exciting and rewarding. As my clients open to discover the truth of their being, their God-particle nature that is Spirit and love, the world is seen in a different light. All that is learned in this team effort is about all people—not just about substance abuse, chemical dependency or other destructive behaviors.

Since 1991, I have been in the business of running a residential treatment program for up to 30 people based on a holistic, spiritual solution to destructive behaviors and lifestyles. Because I believe that difficulty and change can be facilitated and helped, I myself was helped in the creation of Arizona Pathways of Life, Unity and Love.

I am often asked, "How do you start something like Arizona Pathways?" I don't believe that I started it. It seems as though it started itself through me.

Since childhood, I have always been sensitive to sadness and unhappiness in people around me. My father used to ask me why I was always hanging with the "underdogs." He told me that they would drag me down. Yet, my father was probably the first "underdog" that I was attracted to. He was one of the unhappiest people I ever knew. As a result, everyone in my family was pretty miserable.

My father was not an alcoholic, but his mood swings were violent and unpredictable much like those of many alcoholics. I tried hard as a child to bring peace and harmony to a very dysfunctional family. Of course, I was not very successful. My parents were kind, honest and hardworking, but they did not receive the help they needed. This was common in the 1950s and '60s. What wasn't talked about didn't really happen, so everyone pretended that there were no serious problems. Families or individuals certainly did not go to counselors or therapy in my world.

The events of my life, from what I can see now in 2012 at the age of 69, helped set me up for a career in rehabilitation of addicts. I included an autobiography in chapter 10 that describes the conditions I went through, including the navigation of some difficult relationships and a near-death experience. But my career really began when I had the desire to fix the trouble I saw and felt in my family of origin. It was hard work, and I was not successful. At first.

I couldn't fix my family so I found love and support in the

families of friends. I married my first husband not just because I loved him, but I loved his family. I believed that I would be able to create a family like his. Unfortunately, even though I dated him for three years, I didn't know that he had a separate life. After he took me home during those dating years, he would go out drinking with friends who I didn't know. Once we were married, he couldn't take me home and I became aware of his other life. As the time passed he drank more and more and became violent. I left him several times but he always convinced me it would be better and I would return. I tried to be the perfect wife and mother to our son. He stopped drinking for a year and I thought everything was going to be perfect, but it started all over and he became so violent that I was afraid for my life and afraid for my little boy. I finally divorced him.

So, I couldn't fix my family of origin, and now I couldn't fix my husband and my marriage. I didn't realize it at that time, but I needed to understand that I couldn't fix anyone.

I kept looking for answers. I went to many different churches, took classes, read books, attended retreats and seminars. I met and married my current husband in 1967. He adopted my son and we raised another son together along with two children from his first marriage. Life has been interesting, challenging and eventful, but never violent and frightening. We have learned a lot and we keep learning.

In 1981 we moved to Phoenix from Flagstaff and I started an employment agency. One day I was talking with a client about job opportunities and he asked me if I was a "religious scientist." I asked him what that was and why he'd asked. He said that I talked like one. Then he told me about the church he attended. I visited his church and was very pleased that what they taught made perfect sense to me. So, I began taking all of the classes that were offered. It was like being so very hungry and finding the best food possible.

After completing all of the required classes I became a "Licensed Practitioner," which is a spiritual counselor. The license was issued by The United Church of Religious Science. Still wanting to know more about life, God, spirit and love, I began attending seminary classes with Lola Mays, D.Div., at the Living Bible Center in Mesa, Arizona. Dr. Lola insisted that I accept ordination in 1990 after completing that training. I took those classes for my own personal growth, not planning on being a minister, but I found out later that this was the perfect outcome.

A few months later, I was helping to present a women's retreat for the church I attended. At this retreat, I was participating in a meditation and visioning activity. The facilitator led us through a relaxing exercise and then said, "If anyone has an inspiration relating to their purpose or next step in their personal growth, just stand up and express it to the group."

I found myself standing us and saying, "I'm going to start a church."

She asked, "When are you going to start this church?"

I answered, "the first Sunday in July." This was the third week of June. I thought, "Who said this, who stood me up and said this?" It seemed absolutely crazy, but on the first Sunday in July 1990, we held our first church service.

I became a licensed practitioner in 1988, and at the beginning of the new church in 1990, a close friend who also was a fellow practitioner, Rev. Roberta Croddy, D.D., and I created a spiritual counseling center called The Wholeness Center in a small building on the church property. I had discovered that my younger-by-19 years sister, who had recently moved to Arizona, was suffering from anorexia and bulimia. She was skeletal, very sick and miserable. I didn't know anything about eating disorders so I found all the information I could and I talked with everyone who was supposed to be expert about eating disorders. Without thousands of dollars in savings or insurance coverage, we could find nothing to help her. So, we worked on her with the spiritual principles that we had learned as practitioners. She did improve and became healthier. Her story is long and interesting enough to be a book of its own.

Dr. Croddy and I learned a lot by working together through trial and error. Soon we attracted several other clients who were struggling with eating disorders. We developed an outpatient program and worked with them and they all experienced improvement. We made progress but did not find perfection.

We learned that outpatient therapy was not enough. We were given the use of another building, so we opened a four-bed residential program to address eating disorders from a holistic (spirit, mind, body and emotion) approach. While working with these clients we began to understand that most eating disorders are a form of addiction, and if the eating disorder was controlled, other addictive behaviors appeared. Relationship addiction, sex addiction, alcoholism and drug abuse showed up in our clients.

One day, a couple of guys came to visit one of the girls in our program. One was her boyfriend, the other who I'll call Mike, was his friend and was just providing transportation. While the boyfriend was visiting his girlfriend, Mike talked with me about his own experience with addiction and the work I was doing. I was feeling full of mischief and felt I could really have some fun with this traditional "disease concept, Twelve Step" person. Amazingly as I shared with him my "spiritual" perception of addictions, he agreed with me. So after that conversation, every time Mike brought his friend over to visit the girlfriend, Mike and I would share our thoughts and ideas about addictions and life in general.

Shortly after meeting Mike, I had the opportunity to use a larger complex to offer our program. Mike agreed to be the on property manager. He had seven years of sobriety and had worked in a detox program and a residential treatment program. So Mike had the experience of his own addiction and recovery and also of working in a treatment program. Mike was the expert. I was the novice. This was the beginning of Arizona Pathways of Life, Unity and Love's residential program for freedom from addictions. This also was my school for education from the master teachers who showed up to teach me what it is really like to become addicted to chemicals and other destructive lifestyles.

In my prayers, meditations and journaling, I was asking God: "What am I here for? What do You want me to do?" When Arizona Pathways evolved, I questioned God about why I would be one to help these people. I had never been addicted and I couldn't help my ex-husband, or my father. Why me? Why this?

Then I felt the answer. It was because I knew that I didn't know how to free them, because I hadn't been addicted myself, because I hadn't taken formal training to treat addictions. I didn't have to unlearn. I was open to learn from the real experts, the addicted themselves. I had the desire to help underdogs and the misunderstood since I was a child, and I still have that strong desire. I have always invited challenges. I thrive on the potential to solve the most difficult situations. I have always been hungry and thirsty for wisdom and understanding. I have always been curious, always desiring to know more about God. I have always been able to see the good in everyone and in every situation, sometimes not immediately but always eventually.

Perhaps I do what I do because I *must* do it. Maybe this is what is meant by the term, "a calling."

Chapter 2:

Addiction is Natural, Treatment is Too

THERE ARE OVERWHELMING NUMBERS OF people struggling with addictions.

There are overwhelming numbers of people who love the people who are struggling with addictions. There are overwhelming numbers of people working to help people become free from addictions.

And we have a society where we say the number one problem is substance abuse or drug addiction.

This book is meant to address all of these people with a broad and accurate understanding of what's happening, and my thoughts about how we can lovingly support, heal and resolve the crisis in which we find ourselves. I believe that everyone who reads it with an open mind will find something to help them understand more about their own addictions or lack of addictions, about other people's addictions, and that no matter their life situation, they can become a part of helping to solve the problem instead of contributing to it.

I'm writing this book to share what I've learned since 1987, and am still learning, about substance abuse, drugs, alcohol, relationship and food addictions. I've had the best teachers possible: not Ph.D. professors but my clients. These wonderful and courageous people have provided me with private lessons because so few choose to learn directly from these master teachers. I encourage others to be willing to learn what I've learned from them by reading this book.

Everyone I know and talk with has someone in his or her family or social circle who is suffering or has suffered from addictions to chemicals of some kind. This is true in my family, too. I personally know the pain, fear and frustration of living with someone who is destroying their life, often lying, stealing and otherwise harming us or breaking our hearts as we witness their self-destruction. I've tried desperately to find help for loved ones who finally asked for help to stop their pain, their insanity—so I know how hard it is to find that help, especially if you don't have money or insurance to pay for it.

As an ordained minister, I often use religious terms including the word God or Spirit in my communications. Everyone comes to an understanding of what God and Spirit is on his or her own. While it is about spirituality, it's not about religion. To me, religion is how you may choose to practice your spirituality. I have attended churches of most denominations and have studied others. I was raised in an evangelical Christian religion, my most recent studies were in Religious Science, and I completed ministerial training at the Living Bible Center in 1990. I respect all religions and teachers and choose to keep my mind open to expanding ideas. I invite you to do the same. Please take what you can use and just let the rest go without judgment.

The name of our church, Arizona Pathways Church of Life, Unity and Love, says it all for me. Whatever word you may use, if it contains those qualities, this book is for you.

Addicts and love

Addiction is related to love or lack of it, and that brings up the question of what is real love? We talk about it all the time, and yet to be able to put it into words or to share an understanding seems quite a challenge. The Bible teaches that God is love and that God is spirit. Also it is said that spiritual things cannot be expressed in human language. So that's where the challenge comes from. My understanding of God is that God is power, and, if God is love, then love must be powerful. I believe love is a feeling that connects us to each other, to nature, to puppies and polliwogs. It is the glue of life.

When we watch a movie and get emotional when a character has overcome trauma, that emotion is love. It's stimulated by our inner awareness of our unity of life. When catastrophes, such as floods, tornadoes, fires and earthquakes happen, people rally and support each other. The separation of the economic classes, race, religion, lifestyle all seem to disappear as people join in unity to survive and to rebuild in the face of disaster.

It's fun to be a loving person. It's joyful to help someone that's stuck in the mud, to help a lost child find a parent, to nurse an injured animal to health. To help in any way actually feels good or allows us to feel high on happiness. Each of us has certain talents, skills and ideas that are only valuable if they are utilized for the good of all. Love is expressing both the giving of our gifts and the receiving of the gifts of others. Love is what we are.

Unfortunately, this perception of love is not always taught. Often we encourage our children to find their particular talent, strength, skill, and then to find a way to use it to become prosperous. Our goal is not to feel good—is not the feel good that is the result of using our special gifts to the benefit of all, but to use our special gifts to compete with others: to earn more to have more and to be more, none of which makes us feel good for very long. In this way of living, we are constantly striving for more or better, and as a result, our natural craving to feel good becomes an obsession which can drive us to drugs, alcohol, gambling, eating disorders, to the point of addiction or dependency, when all we really want is to feel good.

Loving God, loving ourselves as God's children and loving one another is the only authentic high or feel-good that can fulfill us and provide joy and peace in our daily life experiences. Love is that inner desire for wanting the best for ourselves and for others, that desire is free only when we're not afraid for ourselves, free when we know God is the power in our lives, free when we know we are all a part of the whole expression of God as the human family, free when we know that our good and another's good is one, is God.

How often do addicts feel good by sharing their gifts with someone else, and how often do they feel good by receiving the benefit of someone else's talents that are freely shared? I'm afraid the answer to both of those questions is 'hardly ever.' Addicts are so busy serving their god—heroin, alcohol, cocaine, pot, meth, sex, food, so forth—that they miss out on the natural highs that can be found in the non-addicted side of life. They are so busy trying to get high that they eliminate the real high of giving and sharing. The end result is that everything is taken from them.

Or it can be the other way around—they feel like nothing was GIVEN to them early on and they are busy trying to fill that hole. They do not know what the "everything" is that has been "taken" from them because the "everything" was not given in the first place.

Many people think that addicts are just self-serving, irresponsible, useless burdens to society. Because of this perception, they don't want to help them. They don't believe they can or will change. This incurable disease they have is eventually terminal. But then again, life in the human form always terminates, doesn't it? Because the labels related to their behavior and/or other mental health labels always identify addicts and alcoholics, society has a tendency to see them within that limitation. While generally accepting that they are victims of a disease, they are still not viewed as fellow humans, part of our whole human family that are worth accepting for who they are, beyond their disease.

How often have you thought or heard someone say, "They deserve what they get," meaning homelessness, incarceration, poverty, loneliness and death. Do they deserve self-loathing? Do they deserve the shunning they receive from others? Are they not more than their destructive behaviors? Are they not our brothers and sisters, created by the same Creator, loved as much as anyone by God? If you are asking these questions, it is time to see addiction in another way—as something that comes naturally to human beings—not as an illness, not as something to be punished, not as a problem to navigate through layers of social programs, but something to be treated with as much compassion as is possible.

Addiction is natural

The criminal justice system views addiction as a crime. To the extent that addiction is an underlying problem in the commission of many crimes, that's understandable. But when punishment becomes the treatment for addiction, it doesn't work and mostly makes the problem worse.

The medical and mental health system sees addiction as an illness. The experience of chemical dependency, including use, long term effects and withdrawal, certainly looks and acts like illness. And classifying addiction as an illness is also a means for medical treatment to receive payment via insurance plans. But treating addiction as illness creates it's own problems. Treating addiction and withdrawal with legal drugs is ineffective and dangerous.

Many established treatment programs view addictions as incurable diseases, which also stops short of addressing the truth behind it. A person's experience of being "powerless over my addictions" is interpreted as an experience that holds them apart from the rest of humanity, an insurmountable difference between them and "normal" people.

Drugs themselves are often seen as the enemy by society as a whole—such as in the "war on drugs"—as if drugs have some kind of intrinsic power to draw people to them and addict them against their will. This view allows the individual to place blame on an inanimate substance for their situation, rather than face the painful and complicated truth of addiction.

The fact that society throws money at the war on drugs is an example of how financial resources are misused. This money would be better spent on treatment centers such as Arizona Pathways, where the truth of addiction is handled in a compassionate and supportive manner.

But if addiction is not a crime, if it's not a disease, if it isn't a matter of evil substances attacking us, what is it?

I think it is a natural response to a profound, unmet need.

Why is addiction natural?

It seems that everyone has a need, a strong desire to feel good, to be "high," or free from pain, whether physical, mental, or emotional. Much of our human endeavor is an effort to feel good. This need is a natural drive within everyone, one that we are born with, and one that can actually assist us as spiritual beings. We are always seeking the peace, joy and love that arise from being aware of our spiritual nature.

Most faiths agree that we are individual, unique expressions of the Creator, or what I call God. This thing I call God is the source and basis of all. According to the Bible, God is a spirit, we are the image and likeness of God, and therefore our true essence is spirit, as expressed in physical or human form. Scriptures also identify God as love, so our nature is to give and receive unconditional love. Many people do not understand how human love can be unconditional, but it is a simple concept. It is love without attachment or judgment and it is done in a space of freedom that we all can choose through the power of our own attitude. We are created equal in value but individual in expression.

I believe that people caught up in the human experience of addiction to destructive chemicals and/or behaviors actually are responding to that basic need for this love energy that I call God. Not understanding their true nature as spiritual beings, they seek to satisfy this very real need by craving things of this physical world. Many people find less destructive behaviors or things to become addicted to, but nonetheless, they are distracted from the real causes for the cravings. Addiction to food, work, shopping, caffeine, tobacco, being sick, needing to be in a relationship, vanity, money, TV, video games, exercise—all normal parts of healthy human living when experienced in moderation, yet destructive when they become obsessive or addictive.

Let me present it in a non-religious way. What is the difference between you, me and a corpse? What is that invisible energy or source of life that animates our physical bodies? It's not the brain, or the heart, because a corpse has all of its physical parts, doesn't it? I'm talking about that invisible yet powerful life source when I refer to God or Spirit. Also think about the feeling of being loved, desiring love or loving someone else. That feeling that we all crave, the highest of highs—that is our nature and I call it God or Spirit Nature. Many of us have been hurt by those we expected to be our source of love and have hardened our hearts or numbed out the desire with drugs, alcohol, food, etc.

But we still crave love (the source of which is God) even

through our resistance. We may also fear it because we thought it came from outside ourselves, from other people, from parents, friends, lovers—and many of us felt we had lost it, or maybe have become convinced that we are not lovable because of our experiences of unmet expectations of others.

Love is our nature, and our creator is its source, and we are created dependent on it. To use the language of addiction, we "crave" it, needing our daily or moment-to-moment "fix" or we go into "withdrawal," a desperate feeling of lacking what we need. When in withdrawal we seek a substitute, the object of our substance addiction, until we have created more bondage, lost more freedom.

It's not a quick fix. Unlearning takes time and work, and for each individual it is a path of personal discovery. Old habits and the beliefs that support them must be relinquished. New beliefs must be understood, and a new way of living takes much practice until it becomes habitual. We each experience life according to our beliefs. Our self-identity is based on what we believe to be true about ourselves. To be free from the bondage of chemicals or destructive, obsessive behaviors, we must be free to believe in our own natural state of being, which is spiritual offspring of the Creator.

I've observed how real the craving for love is in the individuals who come to our program—even as they struggle with abstinence from their drug of choice, even when they are attempting to satisfy the mutual craving with chemicals. Animals, pets, are part of the program at Arizona Pathways, and I notice how most people really absorb attention from these animals, how they enjoy the touching, the playing and the caring for these pets. Dogs and cats give freely of their attention without judgment, their touching and playing. They are pure expressions of unconditional love, and as such they help soothe the fear and hurt in humans. The power of animal—human interaction is a gift from God!

One of my master teachers, Eddie, demonstrated this power of bonding with animals. When I first met Eddie, one of our first clients, I felt intimidated. Eddie was from Brooklyn, Italian, an ex-con with tattoos and dark, piercing eyes. To me he looked like a gangster and I had never been around anyone like him. He identified himself as a dope fiend or a junkie. Eddie had been addicted to heroin since he was 14 and he was now 39. He had served time in Rikers Island Prison in New York when he was 17. He had been to a treatment program in Hawaii, met his ex-wife and became a father. His wife stayed clean and sober but Eddie continued to use drugs. He came to us out of jail, on probation for five years. He had been arrested in a DEA sting while attempting to buy drugs.

Now another client, a young smartass kid, bought a pet rat from the pet store. This kid lived on the second floor of our center. One day he thought it would be funny to throw the rat out of the window. Eddie heard the laughter relating to the episode, went outside to investigate, and rescued the rat. The kid that threw the rat out the window then attempted to reclaim it. I thought Eddie was going to kill him.

Eddie adopted the rat and named him Baby. Baby slept with Eddie and rode on his shoulder during the day. Eddie was very gentle and caring with Baby. About three years later, Eddie came to talk to me about Baby. He was very upset, those eyes that had seemed so piercing and cold when I first met Eddie were now softened and brimming with tears. Baby was sick. His eye was bulging and he wasn't eating or sleeping. Eddie took Baby to the vet and unfortunately found that Baby had a brain tumor and had to be put to sleep. Eddie cried and was very sad for some time.

But something real was happening to Eddie and it was good.

After all the years of not feeling because of heroin, Eddie was feeling the loss of something he loved. But Eddie didn't believe that he could survive the pain of losing Baby. He went out and got heroin.

After using the heroin to treat his grief, Eddie did something he had never done before—he told on himself. He came to me and told me what he had done. The normal response of a program would be to kick him out, at least until he could provide a clean drug test. I surprised Eddie with my response. I thanked him for telling the truth and told him I understood that he didn't know how to experience the pain of his loss without drugs. I acknowledged that he was making progress toward his freedom from the bondage of drug addiction. We talked about being thankful for the experience of Baby. Eddie began to see things differently, so he could begin to live differently. Later, Eddie adopted a stray cat and named him Baby.

Eddie changed in positive ways because of the unconditional love of Baby the rat and he found the ability to survive loss of one pet and accept the love of another. Eddie demonstrated to all of us that the source of love flows through all of creation and it flows continuously and eternally. Eddie was learning about the natural craving for love that is in every one of us. The loss of the unconditional love pets provide is a way of preparing us for what we experience as greater losses such as family members, friends, years of our life, finances, homes, freedom and much more. Yes, Eddie was just beginning. He had lots of losses to feel in order to experience his own power, to begin to understand that it really is "better to have loved and lost than never to have loved at all."

Just like the unconditional love of animals helps us to recognize our natural need for love and affection, our physical body craves what it requires to be healthy. Think of feeling thirsty when we need water, hungry for protein, sugar or salt when our body needs it. This is similar to the natural craving for love (Spirit/God) that causes people to seek "a fix." Many people yearn to find relief for this craving of love with something outside of themselves. Unfortunately, drugs, alcohol, pills—counterfeits in the beginning—seem to fulfill the craving, only to create bondage and destruction.

Treatment is continual

The craving for a spiritual awareness, connection and expression is very real and everyone is born with it. This craving's purpose is to inspire us to find and experience the "fix." It is just as real as the craving for drugs, food, sex...whatever we become obsessed with. When we are unfulfilled, we are in a state of desire of wanting, of needing relief.

This quote from Charles Borden's book *Down by the River* expresses this perfectly:

Besides control, besides trust, there is the matter of wanting something.

Never want something. If you want something, other people can feed your desire. And as they feed you and you consume what they offer, they take control.

This is an example of addiction and obsession, of giving away your own power. But when we realize what we really crave, really want, really need, is a spiritual connection, we understand this is something already available and there is no person, no "dealer," who can feed us spiritual substance. We only need to learn that we need it, what it is and how to experience it. It is always invisible but sometimes it is expressed in nature, music, art, friendship, companionship—all that causes us to feel good, safe, joyful, peaceful, contented, etc.—without taking from or hurting us or anyone else.

When people have this realization and are no longer found

"wanting" they are no longer addicts, as in the idea that "once an addict/alcoholic, always an addict/alcoholic." It is interesting that when a smoker quits smoking they are quickly recognized as a non-smoker, socially, medically and by insurance companies. This is true even though many non-smokers return to smoking after various periods of time as a non-smoker. Many smokers quit many times. We should give the same encouragement to those addicted to drugs. Becoming a non-addict versus a "recovering addict" seems much more positive. In fact, not labeling people based on their personal experience at all is an even better idea.

The cure for emptiness is fulfillment. Emptiness is craving. Fulfillment is seeing ourselves as spiritual offspring of God/ Spirit, of love. Accepting this truth causes us to feel fulfilled and loved and allows us to let that love flow toward others. When we are fulfilled in this way, cravings for substitutes diminish. This process can take a while, with fits and starts, fears arising and the ego fighting the progress, but it can and does happen.

We must not only know that we are of God, but we must continue to seek a higher understanding of God as life, love, power, intelligence, creativity and to experience God everywhere, at all times, and that there is no separation between God and us. As we love, work, play and live we are experiencing this Divinity within us.

At Arizona Pathways we don't refer to ourselves or others as addicts and/or alcoholics. Our understanding is that addiction to drugs or alcohol is real human experience but it is never the whole truth about what someone is. We see everyone as a child of God, a brother or sister. Eddie, as related in the story about the pet rat, said to me, "I was never told that I was a child of God before. I always believed that I was a junkie, a loser." The understanding that we are all the beloved offspring of the loving source of life, God, is the truth that sets us free.

Our natural craving is for unconditional love, also known as Spirit and God.

Crimes are committed under the influence of addiction, but addiction itself is not a crime.

People experiencing substance abuse or who are in detoxification from substances exhibit behaviors that appear as illness, but they are probably not diseased or mentally ill. Chemical addictions usually also include emotional and psychological addictions. Treatment must address the "whole" person for success.

Most addicts and alcoholics have been experiencing addictions for a long time. Successful treatment usually takes a long time.

Addictions are the experiences of continuing any behaviors knowing that these behaviors will eventually destroy everything we really value, even life.

Craving requires fulfillment. Negative fulfillment is found through the escape destructive behavior offers. Positive fulfillment requires love. It is not easy to figure out how to supply yourself with love. First you have to take a leap of faith and believe that a power greater than your own self loves you. Then you have to learn to love yourself. Then, through your loving behaviors, others will respond to you with love.

The most natural fulfillment for a craving is having an inner feeling of divine unconditional love.

That is why treatment for this natural craving is continual.

Chapter 3:

Experiencing Addiction

IT TAKES WHAT IT TAKES, and however long it takes is however long it takes.

When I answered the phone, the voice sounded familiar, yet I couldn't place it. After hearing, "I'm so glad I still remembered your number after all of this time. How are you?"

I answered, "I'm good. How are you and who are you?"

"This is Troy."

Never give up! Troy's story

It took me a moment because my eldest son is named Troy and I knew this wasn't my son. Then, of course, I knew the Troy who was calling. I remembered that he was one of our very first clients in 1991. He was 28 or 29 at the time, a handsome, strong, intelligent man with a serious alcohol habit and a know-it-all attitude.

Troy always returned to Arizona Pathways between jail, prison, falling in love, relapsing and starting over. He was hardworking, kind, compassionate and likeable. He just couldn't or wouldn't accept that his addiction to alcohol was the beginning of legal problems and participation with heroin and other illegal drugs. He would get several months of sobriety then decide to drink alcohol and start the cycle over and over again. When he finally completed his probation and parole requirements in Arizona, he returned home to Pennsylvania.

After he moved, he called me a couple of times a year. His mother died shortly after he moved home and he told me that he was happy to have been sober during that time. He said his biggest fear was that she would die while he was in jail.

A year passed after that call and then I got a letter from him—from jail. He had gotten a DUI, had been driving with a suspended license and other related charges. This was nothing new—it was Troy's formula for living his life.

In the summer of 2011, he called again to tell me that he was going to marry. He was sober and happy.

A while later he called again. He said, "Something happened to me. I have to tell you about it." Here is what he shared with me:

Everything was great! I had been sober for a year. I had a great job, was planning to marry Ruth. She was perfect for me. We found a home and I was doing maintenance and remodeling it before we moved in. One Friday after work I drank a couple of beers with the guys. Ruth did not know. I handled it just fine—two beers—no big deal. Then on Saturday I went to work on our home. I decided I could get a six-pack and have a few beers throughout the day, while I worked. The next thing I knew, it was Sunday morning, and Ruth was shaking me and screaming. I looked around and saw the place littered with empty beer cans, vodka bottles and a big mess. Once I was awake and alert, I tried to apologize to Ruth. She said that she could not live with this and left.

I was brokenhearted, and hung over. So I did what I always did—got more alcohol. Then I called my uncle who lived in New Orleans and told him my tale of woe. He invited me to stay with him and get a new start. He told me that there were lots of construction jobs and pretty girls. So I packed up my stuff and drove to Louisiana all the while drinking vodka, smoking pot and shooting heroin.

It was a small town in Maryland where I stopped to get a room and once I checked in, I went out to get more vodka. On the way back, I got into a car accident. Another driver failed to stop and t-boned my truck. I was thrown out and banged up but not seriously injured so I just left the scene and walked back to the motel.

The police found me, probably because I had left a receipt from the motel in the truck. They arrested me for leaving the scene and I was sentenced to a year in prison but was released after nine months. While in prison I sobered up and called Ruth. She helped retrieve my truck and possessions, then she wrote me a "Dear John" letter. I felt bad for hurting her and was very depressed, but I managed to stay clean and sober while in prison, even though I knew how to get drugs. Instead, I read a lot of self help books, books on motivation and spirituality. Some of the titles I'd remembered seeing while at Arizona Pathways.

When I got released, I called Ruth. She told me that she'd moved on and there was no turning back. I told her that I understood, apologized again, wished her the best, hung up the phone then went out and bought a bottle of vodka.

I looked at that bottle for a long time. I thought about what my life would be like if I had stayed sober. For the first time in my life, I threw away the bottle—without ever taking a sip. I walked away from that trashcan, feeling lost, depressed and wondering what to do next.

When I was released from prison, they'd given me a list of programs for homeless people, halfway houses and shelters, so I went to a phone and started calling. A homeless shelter took me in and I felt safe and supported there because it reminded me of Arizona Pathways.

After a few days, the director sent me to a social service agency to see if I could get any benefits. I rode in a van to the agency and the driver told me to call for a pick up when I was finished. After spending a few hours filling out paperwork and talking with a caseworker, I walked to a liquor store and bought a half pint of vodka. I called for a pick up but was told that it would take a few hours, so I went to a restaurant, sat in a corner booth and ordered a cup of coffee. I was in no hurry because I figured I had some serious drinking to do.

I took the bottle out of my pocket and looked at it. Suddenly, I felt very uncomfortable. When I looked up, I saw eight pairs of eyes staring at me. I took a few sips of coffee, stared at the bottle, then looked back at my audience. I felt something happening inside and after what seemed to be forever, I looked back at the crowd and said, "I know that I don't need this. In fact, I know that I don't want this."

I got up and put the bottle in the trash. Everyone cheered and clapped. I sat down, and although I was smiling there were tears in my eyes.

Then the van arrived and I went back to the shelter and told the director what had happened. She said, "You are on your way!" In that moment I finally understood what I learned at Arizona Pathways about life, unity and love.

Those people at the restaurant—all strangers—cared about me. They really connected with me. Because of the way they treated me, I started going to AA. I started to ask for help. I now accept that asking for help is a sign of courage and not of weakness.

Troy's story made me very happy. Now that he is in mid-life, he finally recognizes his purpose in life and I believe he will make it his mission to help others who face a struggle similar to the one he faced—breaking free of the bondage of addiction.

Don't ever give up on yourself or your loved ones. It takes what it takes. And, it takes as long as it takes, as Troy's story shows.

What it is like to be an addict

As I work with and talk with drug addicts and alcoholics, I witness what certainly appears to be insanity—intelligent, talented and attractive people giving up everything to continue to abuse chemicals. They give up their jobs, their homes, families, cars, possessions, money, health, teeth, self-respect, freedom and anything except their lover, their god, which happens to be drugs or alcohol or destructive behavior. They actually miss almost all of normal life experience in exchange for a "high" or numbness. They're rather like zombies, the living dead. They violate other people's rights. They violate their own boundaries and values. They live to chase and use, chase and use. They spiral down and down into a black pit. It seems that there is no way out.

If you're not one of them, it's very difficult to understand. It's very difficult to have compassion when they appear to be so unwilling to change. They make thousands of promises, but they break them all. I think most of us "non-addicts" react in frustration, if we have any real interest in them at all. For those who love an addict, to stand by and watch them suffer is one of the most difficult things for anyone to have to witness.

But let's open our hearts and minds and see if we can make some sense of it. Let's look at this theory that addiction is natural in a little more detail, and try to understand what life is like from the perspective of the addicted person.

Can you remember being so thirsty for a drink of water that you just couldn't think of anything else? If you can't remember an actual experience of this incredible thirst, just imagine that you have been walking for miles down a dusty road on a hot, summer day, and you're lost. Somehow, you missed the sign, and you've wandered off. Your canteen is empty. You start thinking it's dry, you're hot and there's no place to get a drink. All you can think about is water—cool, clear water. You become so obsessed that you stumble, stagger, fall, and get up, only to fall again. You are afraid. You have to have water. Perhaps you will die if you don't get it.

Now, someone approaches you and begins to lecture about your foolishness, being out here lost in the heat without water. Can you hear him? Do you think he cares about you? Why doesn't he just shut up or give you a drink of water?

Now someone else joins you and says he'll give you some water if you'll give him your shoes. So, of course, you do, and he gives you a few drops of water. Oh, you need more! Now he wants your hat; then he wants your shirt, your pants, everything, and you give it all just for a few more drops.

Suppose you really don't know you need water. Perhaps you always drink lemonade, and when your canteen is empty, you become obsessed with lemonade. The story would be the same, except you would really lose, because with all the lemonade in the world, you still would die of thirst for water, because water is really what you need.

Chemical or behavioral addiction is being obsessed with a real need and believing that the need can be filled with a substance—a substance which never really fulfills the craving, but which destroys the life in an attempt to find fulfillment.

The addicted population has great survival skills. They utilize their talents of perseverance, salesmanship, creativity and charm to stay alive. They manage to find food and shelter at minimum and sometimes enjoy lavish lifestyles at maximum. And they continue to find the means to acquire the substances of their dependency. Yes, they usually end up lying, cheating and stealing to accomplish this. Even though they are surviving they are filled with fear, guilt and shame. Because of these feelings, they feel that they are failures, unworthy and unlovable.

I believe that we create our life experiences based on what

we think and believe about ourselves and the world we live in. If this is true, the addicted are not capable of thriving in their perceptions of themselves. Sharing life with them, I recognize that they have practically no coping skills in dealing with "normal" life challenges. Most of their chemical dependency is based on the desire to "not feel." Drugs and alcohol create an illusion in the addict's mind that they are invincible so life's challenges are not of concern to them. Most people learn about cause and effect by finding solutions to problems. Those who are addicted refuse to be consciously aware of their problems. No wonder they "like" the effects of their substances of choice.

Many of our clients come from wonderful families. But sometimes these wonderful families are overprotective and over-indulging. Some people grow up in this kind of environment and mature as wonderful, kind, successful and happy adults. Unfortunately some individuals don't mature emotionally. They expect the world to treat them just as their families do and they don't know what to do when it doesn't happen that way. "Using" is a way to not feel. It is a way not to accept responsibility for their actions. This becomes a way of life. When parents can't bear to watch their children experience the consequences of their choices and actions, kids do not develop coping skills that prepare them for life's challenges.

The other extreme is families that model irresponsible actions as acceptable. This environment also fails to prepare children to cope with life experiences. Thankfully, most people figure it out regardless of their family of origin.

No matter what type of family of origin they came from, those who show up at Arizona Pathways are filled with fear. Some of the main reasons they ask for help are that they feel that they have run out of options for survival. This is often referred to as "reaching their bottom." Once they find food and shelter, they focus on their fear of withdrawal and of life without the substance. The fear of detox is magnified in the mind of the addicted. Even though they may have gone through it many times previously, they convince themselves that it is almost impossible to accomplish. For this reason many leave detox facilities against medical advice. Then they are facing the fear of not finding a way to obtain the substance that they need to be okay. For those who complete detoxification, the next fear is one of relapse, guilt, shame and unworthiness. Because they have been told that they are addicts/alcoholics, they perceive all situations as though this were true. It is understandable that the ability to believe that life can be experienced clean and sober is impossible.

Soon after detox they begin to feel as though something is missing. This is because something *is* missing. They have lost their best friend—the friend they have depended on for a long time. When faced with feelings, responsibilities and decisions, the newly clean and sober person doesn't know what to do or how to respond to life situations. What most of us learned gradually in the process of growing up, they didn't learn. We learned through actions and reactions, choices and consequences, trial and error. The addicted learned to run away through chemicals. Now as adults life is frightening for them.

Many addicted individuals don't want to feel the pain of remembering trauma and/or sexual, physical and emotional abuse. This is true for a high percentage of females. Many males have also been abused. It is a process to learn to accept past abuses as seeds of strength instead of excuses for weakness. Military veterans also often turn to drugs and/or alcohol to block out flashbacks of violence and terror. Traumatized individuals require lots of support and patience. For most of them it takes a long time in a safe, nurturing and supportive environment.

The most important thing we can offer is this truth:

everyone is a child of God, a spiritual being. No one is what he has experienced. It usually takes some time in an environment that reinforces this fact for it to become a personal belief and conviction. Also proper nutrition is necessary to restore physical and mental health and normal chemical balances. When clients begin to believe that they really are spiritual beings having a human experience, they respond to everything in a more positive way. In our humanness, we all live according to our beliefs and understanding.

Thank God we can acquire more information and change what we think and believe. I observe that the fear is being replaced with faith when the clients reach out to help each other. They welcome new clients and help them to acclimate to the Pathways environment. They volunteer to help the community and the neighborhood. The true Child of God expresses and shares their individual skills and talents. They begin to feel good about themselves. I see the good (I see God) in them long before they see it in themselves. I do my best to help them recognize how lovable they really are. This awareness is their pathway to freedom from the pain of their past.

Many family members have banned a member from their home, or said, "You can't use here. We don't want to see you if you're using drugs or alcohol." Can you imagine being so thirsty yet being told you could never drink any lemonade in their home? You're dying of thirst; there are faucets everywhere, but you can't drink lemonade in their home and you can't be around them if you drink lemonade. You can only drink water if you are with them, but you don't want water. It would be very stressful. For someone addicted to a substance like lemonade, it feels similar to non-addicts being denied a natural need, such as water for thirst.

Yet we have no tolerance at all for them using their chemicals, which have become as normal to them as water is to us. This description is not meant to excuse substance abuse, but just a way to describe it in terms we can relate to, and maybe to help the addicted person to understand it.

Now, suppose you live in a very poor country, where you actually dig in the garbage to find something to eat. Sometimes you eat bugs, roots, and leaves, whatever you can find. Then suddenly you are brought to the United States and find yourself in an alley behind the kitchen of one of our wonderful, fancy resorts. You see men pushing big, plastic barrels out the door, leaving them by the curb. You open them to find an amazing feast of meats, breads, vegetables, fruits and pastries. Of course, they're all discards from the plates of others, but you don't know that. It seems like heaven is right out at the curb for you. And when people show up and tell you to get out of that garbage, you think they are crazy! And if they are nice and offer to bring you to a place where you can get a fresh meal directly from a kitchen, are you willing to leave the barrels of garbage to go? Or are you afraid to leave the treasures that you had found to check out that unknown dining room? You realize that the big barrels are placed out there every day so at least and at last you can eat to your heart's content. Surely, you can't risk losing this!

So addiction is like this. Addicts find a substance or behavior that fills the emptiness—the need for love and peace that we all have. They are afraid to let go of their garbage for fear of the return of the hunger and not finding a better fulfillment. But, what if they give up their drug or behavior of choice in exchange for a doctor-prescribed drug to help them recover and after taking it for a period of time are pronounced healed?

Have they really solved their addiction problem?

Here is one client's description about being a heroin addict. Ted used alcohol, pills and drugs recreationally starting in his teens. For Ted, becoming chemically dependent was a subtle process. He said one day he felt like he had ingested a larva from heroin. The larva had gone through his bloodstream and attached itself to his brain, low in the back of his head. Then the larva started feeding on his brain. It would gnaw and gnaw until he could think of nothing else. The only way to stop the feeling of the larva chewing on his brain was to use heroin. After he injected the drug, the larva quit and he would experience the euphoria of the drug and relief from the gnawing need–only to have it start again a few hours later. The more he fed the larva to get it to stop gnawing on his brain, the bigger and stronger it seemed to be and the more it tormented him. His life became about feeding the larva. He said he knew the only way to become free was to stop feeding the larva until it died of starvation, but the torment of the gnawing was unbearable.

He tried methadone and pills as a substitute but this never satisfied the larva. He began to shoplift Levi jeans from stores to sell to support his drug addiction. Finally, after several arrests for shoplifting, he was sent to prison for five years. When he was released to Arizona Pathways he had still been "feeding the larva" because there was plenty of "larva food" in prison. Other heroin addicts I've talked to agreed that Ted's description of heroin addiction is a good one.

One reason it is so difficult to discontinue using heroin is because in addition to the sensation of something chewing on your brain, heroin withdrawal is similar to being very sick with a severe flu. Symptoms of chills, runny nose, fever, nausea, aches and pains, stomach cramps, muscle cramps, restless legs and the worst symptom, insomnia. One of the greatest challenges is the fact that opiate withdrawal is so miserable and just a little bit of an opiate ingested takes all the sick away immediately. How difficult would it be to resist making a call to have a "fix" delivered to you if you were the one suffering in withdrawal?

In many clients I see that in addition to the drug of choice, they become addicted to the excitement of scoring the drugs, of creating ways to fund the addiction and outsmarting medical doctors. Those who use drugs intravenously often get addicted to the process of "cooking up the drug" and "shooting up the drug." These "sub-addictions" add to the difficulty of obtaining freedom from the addiction. Imagine how it feels to someone with low self-esteem to know he outsmarted a doctor who is held in high esteem, what an ego boost this can be. Also, someone who was never popular can become very sought after when they are the person who knows where and how to obtain the drugs.

How Arizona Pathways sees the addict

At Arizona Pathways we help people with addictions to recognize what appear to be "payoffs" of their destructive lifestyles. We know that what they really need to boost their self-esteem and to find excitement and adventure in their lives is to know who and what they really are. The reality of every person is the fact that we all are individual and unique expressions of the Creator and to know that this presence and power is always within them. Respect will be a natural result of living in this awareness. The ability to learn self-control and to have self-responsibility is probably the best goal of the recovered addict.

At Arizona Pathways, we often talk someone who is skeptical of "the Creator" into recovery. We say things like, "I realize that you may not want to believe in a Creator. I realize that you do not believe in the concept of God. I understand and witness that you are not capable of having trust and faith in the unseen. You are unable to make a leap of faith and see God and His work in all that is around you. You are spiritually devoid. But even a rock has its own consciousness! Even water, because of its molecular energy and structure, has its own consciousness! If those things have a consciousness, why do you resist your own consciousness as a developed, thinking human being? It didn't take much for you to give your power to drugs/alcohol. What will it take for you to give your personal power and belief over to a power higher than yourself, sight unseen, that can stay your course, get you out of choppy waters or turbulent air? If you can believe in the power of drugs to make you feel better, what will it take for you to believe that Spirit will TRULY make you feel better, act better?"

The animals we use at Arizona Pathways help teach addicts a sense of love. Sometimes we ask them if they have ever loved anyone. When they say yes (because everyone is given a chance to love at some point) we say if you believe in love then you believe in the Creator because God is love.

Addiction is a natural way of trying to fill a craving for unconditional love. I'm grateful to be aware of my craving for love and not mistake it for a craving for it's weak replacements—not romantic love, but the unconditional love that is everywhere, the love I call God. The feeling of being in the flow of unconditional love is truly getting high. When I get caught up in worldly things I notice that I actually experience withdrawal, a physical discomfort. I need and want to be happy. I need and want to be healthy. I need and want to be with people. I need and want to love them and allow them to love me. I need my regular "fix" of happiness, health and love on a regular basis. I do everything to give and to receive love. I have given up my attachment to material things and behaviors to be free for God's love to flow in my life. This allows me to live in peace and without fear. I cannot survive without love, and I don't know anyone that can or should.

I am saddened that many people feel the same way about their drug or behavior of choice as I feel about love. They are willing to give up everything for it, just like I am willing to give up my attachment to things that get in the way of happiness, health and love. They believe they cannot live without it, or that without it, life wouldn't be worth living—just as I feel about love. The difference is that I have discovered what my true need is, and the fulfillment of my need gives me freedom and joy. The fulfillment of my need does not destroy me in any way. Believing the lie that the craving can be filled with substances leads to bondage and misery. What if society said I had to give up my need for love? Would I rebel? You bet. What if they made it illegal? Would I keep loving and pursuing love anyway? You bet. Of course it would be impossible to outlaw the need or fulfillment for unconditional love because it doesn't come from a source separate from ourselves. We don't break in to other peoples' houses to get it. We don't shoplift it. We don't hoodwink a doctor to get it. We can always find it by going within.

Expressing unconditional love for those caught up in the bondage of destructive substances and/or behavior is key. Holding on to the belief that they are worthy of true love until they can hold on to it for themselves is a way for them to recognize the real craving that drives all other cravings, and experience the peace of feeling loved. This is not to say that we should condone or ignore what they are doing that harms them and all of society, but that we love them in spite of the destructive behavior. We've got to love them, if we want them to be free.

As clients share their experiences related to their drug or behavior of choice, I point out to them how similar their relationships with substances are to a relationship with an abusive lover. Most people can't understand why a victim of domestic violence doesn't just leave that abusive relationship. It's the same reason why drug addicts don't just leave their drug. In an abusive relationship with a person, the victim begins the relationship believing that she or he has found that perfect mate. They've fallen in love and have happy, wonderful times. She relies on her lover to make her feel good, to need her, to love her, to be everything important in her life. Because she is so willing to let him be the most important part of her life, she soon finds that she has lost or given up herself to be loved by him. Now she is vulnerable, and he is taking advantage of that vulnerability.

The person in love with an abuser won't know at first. Things will seem wonderful and the person—due to their inner psychology that dictates their need to be with an abuser—will not know they've chosen an abuser until the abusive behavior begins. Sometimes it is a surprise, they are blindsided and fear leaving because they will be tracked down and harmed further; sometimes they stay because their low self-esteem makes them feel that they deserve the abuse.

Often a substance abuser, themself the victimizer, starts beating—psychologically, physically, spiritually and emotionally—the victim. Men can be abused, but the more common scenario is for men to be the abuser. When the victim is a woman, having no identity of her own anymore if she even had one to start with, feels helpless, hopeless and worthless. Just when she thinks she can't take any more, he promises to change, and often seems to keep that promise, at least for a while. Then it begins again, and it is worse every time. She leaves, he apologizes, promises to change, appears to change, and she returns to the abuse. She leaves him many times, only to be charmed by his promises to change and sincere apologies, and of course the real bait, he says that he just can't live without her.

The cycle continues, no matter the gender. Friends and family give up and no longer offer safety and help to the victim. His or her self-esteem is gone. S/he feels like she deserves nothing better. And, of course, s/he feels responsible to fix the abuser or to save him from himself, until finally she is seriously injured or killed, or her children are hurt, or in so much trouble that she has to choose between them and, of course, many choose their abusive lover. The end result is that everyone loses. This is the same cycle addicts have with their substances or behaviors. They are in an abusive relationship with an abusive lover—thing they love—that eventually takes their freedom, their lives. There's very little difference.

Society has compassion for the battered victim and provides some, although very limited, help. We see the victims of domestic violence as victims worthy of saving, yet these victims play a part in choosing their abusive lover. The addict is very similar. Most people have little or no compassion for these victims. Everyone is seeking something to make them feel good. Feeling good is a natural desire. An abusive lover, whether chemical, human or other, is not an acceptable fulfillment of this desire.

Though I have never been a substance abuser, I have been in abusive relationships. As I learned from the master teachers who arrived at Arizona Pathways as clients, I have related their experiences with substances to my experiences with abusive relationships, and that has helped me to have compassion for them. My first husband was addicted to alcohol and became abusive towards me. I would leave him, and then he would apologize and promise to stop drinking. He would remind me of all the good times we had shared, how much he loved me and I would go back to him. This happened over and over, I don't know how many times. The promises were the same and always broken and the violence continued to escalate.

Finally, I promised God that if I didn't die while experiencing that last beating, I would leave and never return. I kept my agreement with God, but it wasn't easy. I was tempted by the promises and memories of the good times, to give him one more chance—but I didn't. My friends and family were discouraged with my "relapses" into that abusive relationship.

I've shared with clients that I understand my struggle with an abusive husband to be like theirs with their abusive lifestyle. They've agreed. Anything that becomes so important to us that we are willing to be destroyed by it is an abusive relationship, and eventually it will kill us. My experience with obsessive love was an addiction. I was depending on the relationship to "fix" what was really a craving for a connection with spirit, and in the beginning it seemed to fulfill the craving in the same way chemicals do. I was so fortunate to receive insight into this, and I want to do what I can to help others receive the same information and insight.

People caught in the prison of addiction are rarely sentenced by just one substance or behavior. They often experience obsessive or addictive love in addition to substance addiction. To see the difference between obsessive love and true unconditional love takes correct information and practice. As part of the Arizona Pathways treatment program we talk about love all the time, distinguishing between unconditional love and obsessive love. Where obsessive love is a craving that can never be filled, real love connects us to each other. The love we feel in daily life—for our children, our lovers, our friends, our pets—connects us to the unconditional love of spirit. Ordinary daily love is how we practice unconditional love.

My favorite explanation of unconditional love can be found in scripture. From the Bible I use, the George M. Lamsa's Translation from the Aramaic Text, here is 1 Corinthians, chapter 13, verses 1-13:

Though I speak with the tongues of men and of angels, and have not love in my heart, I am become as sounding brass, or a tinkling cymbal. And though I have the gift of prophecy, and understand all mysteries, and all knowledge; and though I have all faith, so that

I could remove mountains, and have not love in my heart, I am nothing.

And though I bestow all my goods to feed the poor, and though I give my body to be burned, and have not love in my heart, I gain nothing.

Love is long-suffering and kind. Love does not envy; love does not make a vain display of itself, and does not boast,

Does not behave itself unseemly, seeks not it's own, is not easily provoked, thinks no evil;

Rejoices not over iniquity, but rejoices in the truth;

Bears all things, believes all things, hopes all things, endures all things.

Love never fails; but whether there be prophecies, they shall fail;

Whether there be tongues, they shall cease; whether there be knowledge, it shall vanish away.

For we know in part, and we prophesy in part. But when that which is perfect is come, then that which is imperfect shall come to an end.

When I was a child, I spoke as a child, I understood as a child; I thought as a child, but when I became a man, I put away childish things.

For now we see through a mirror, darkly; but then face to face; Now, I know in part; but then shall I know even as also I am known. And now abide faith, hope, love, these three; but the greatest of these is love.

It is about all the things you can have and do—but if a person does not have, or feel, love then they have nothing. This passage from the Bible demonstrates the process we experience until we begin to know ourselves—and others—clearly. Learning to love unconditionally requires one to put away judgment, criticism, blame, argument and complaint. At Arizona Pathways, we provide a safe environment for individual growth and expression.

Ellen Gardner, L.I.S.A.C.

We have created a place where unconditional love can be practiced and felt. As our residents learn to live and love themselves and others, mutual trust and respect grows.

Chapter 4:

How to Recognize if Your Loved One is Addicted and What to Do

WHEN YOU FEEL SOMETHING IS not okay with someone you love, especially a family member—you are almost always correct. What can you do in this challenging situation?

The challenge of communication

In many cases, "something has not been okay" for a long time and you've known it. Now is the time for some honest communication. Before you start in, develop an intention of how you'd like the conversation to go. Visualize that both of you will stay calm and rational. Imagine a scenario where your heart is open and their heart is open so that energy is flowing well between the two of you. Imagine also what might happen if anger arises, but imagine that you won't let anything get in the way of conversation until a peaceful solution has been agreed upon.

Once you have set a time for the conversation, offer some standards or define what your boundary is and allow the person who is the addict to offer their version of his or her boundary. For example, agree to take a five-minute break if emotions break out that make conversation impossible. Agree to disagree, but agree to reach a conclusion.

Know that these kinds of conversations with family members

have very high stakes. The stakes are a bit lower with non-family members but keep at the root of each conversation your unconditional love for the addict. A feeling of love should permeate any meeting of this nature. Pay attention to the presence of love. If it feels that it has diminished, take a break and do whatever is necessary to wait for it to come back. Trust that it will.

Prior to confronting your addicted family member or friend, do some work. Observe their behavior, watching close for changes, specifically noticing any significant and abrupt changes in eating, sleeping, hygiene and mood. Other signs of trouble include a change of friends or acquaintances, sudden lack of responsibility with work, school, or family chores. Mood changes might include irritability, defensiveness, argumentativeness, isolating or withdrawing from family and long-term friends. Of course, stealing and lying are very common behaviors for someone abusing chemicals. You may also notice missing prescription medicine from your medicine cabinet or personal room, or missing personal possessions. Other evidence could include small plastic bags, small torn balloons, spoons that are bent and black on the bottom, pill bottles, especially if labels are missing, glass tubes or pipes, cigarette lighters in the room or car of someone who is a non-smoker. Sometimes even something as subtle as a change in choice of music, hairstyle, or clothing can be a cause for concern.

So, if some of these signs are present, does that mean the person may be abusing drugs or alcohol? The answer is probably, but not necessarily. Sometimes the behavior precedes the actual drug use. Sometimes, it's just a behavior, period.

What is the best way to find out which it is? First, create and maintain a safe, loving space to address your concern. Then, state your concerns, your specific reasons for concern, and your unconditional love and support for this person. Also, be prepared to have this person tested, either with a home test (purchased at most drug stores), or at a testing lab in your area that you have located in advance.

Be specific about what support you can and will offer to the person. You may choose to explore some treatment options so you can share that information with this individual. The cost of treatment varies: some insurance companies cover the cost of some programs, and in some areas local services provide treatment for those who meet their criteria. Unfortunately, many people seeking treatment find that they have no financial resources.

Being willing and able to help the abuser you love by footing the bill for his/her treatment is often the only way some people can get help. You may consider hiring a professional interventionist, someone who is experienced in confronting a substance abuser with family and friends whose lives have been impacted by the destructive behavior of the individual of concern.

Most often, even when you lovingly confront a person who is abusing chemicals, their response is defensive. They will deny having a problem. Reassure the person how much you care for them, and request they provide a urine sample for testing. Usually when you intuitively feel, and have observed behavior that validates your concern, the test will be positive. Unless some delay/doctoring has taken place. If it is positive, then you again must reassure the person of your unconditional love and support and discuss how to get past this issue of how seriously involved in addiction is your loved one? At least the situation is out in the open and can be discussed, and a plan of action can be developed and implemented.

What if the person of concern refuses to provide a test sample, and/or becomes angry, and refuses to discuss the matter, or responds in an offensive manner? This is where "tough love" must be expressed. I strongly caution you not to take the love out.

Do not make it all about you. For example, don't ask "what did I do wrong?" or "How can you do this to me, or to your family?"

You didn't do anything to cause someone else to become a substance abuser. Even though you may have contributed to the hurt that the abuser feels and tries to supplant with drugs/alcohol, YOU are not the cause!

Every individual is responsible for themselves and for the choices they make.

This cannot be emphasized enough. Personal responsibility in the place of ability to blame is the junction at which an individual begins to seek help and do the work necessary that goes along with that help.

Although the addicted person may have lied to or stolen from and manipulated you, they really didn't "do it *to* you" or "because of you." I know it causes the one who loves the abuser to be hurt, angry, frustrated and most of all scared, but this is the overall experience of chemical addiction. This unacceptable behavior is a part of it. And, here is the tough part: once it is determined that this loved one's behavior is not acceptable in your home, then you must be tough enough and love them enough to make sure it no longer takes place in your home, the place where such behavior is enabled. This is very hard to do when it is your child or family member, but the most loving thing you can do is keep them out of your home, and thus from being enabled with food and shelter—their most basic needs, until the behavior is no longer in existence.

Why love is not enough

The first couple of years that I worked with people who were addicted, I thought I could just love them enough, support them enough, encourage them enough, teach them enough, provide for them enough, and baby-sit them enough and they would quit abusing chemicals.

I was wrong.

No matter what I did, I have never stopped anyone from using drugs, alcohol or from performing behaviors that are excessive or harmful to others as a way to cover up pain. I probably delayed those actions and behaviors sometimes, but I never stopped anyone.

Recently, I was visiting a family and it became apparent that the eldest son was in trouble with Oxycontin. His mother felt she had to be with him 24 hours a day, every day, to keep him from continuing to abuse these drugs. She was even willing to quit her teaching job to "keep" him from using. I told her that all she would accomplish was more guilt in her son, neglect of the rest of the family, financial stress if she quit her job, damage to her career and stress and sickness for herself. Everyone would suffer and this would probably make it more difficult for the son with the drug problem to find his way out of addiction. *It really hurts to be a parent, friend or family member of anyone addicted to destructive life styles.* As we all talked about the situation, the son agreed to be tested as long as he lived in the home. If he continued to use while living at home, he agreed to go into treatment. If he continued to steal from family members, the police would be called. A lot of tears were shed and a lot of love was shared. The bottom line from his family was "we love you, but you cannot live with us if your behavior hurts you and those you love." It's tough, it's love—and it works, but sometimes it takes a while. It is a process.

I recently had a young man, in his early twenties, come into our program to detoxify from heroin and break free from addiction. He was currently on probation, living with this mother, and was the father of a young son.

The second day he was at our program he disappeared late at night. I called his mother early the next morning. She said that he had come home and was sleeping, and that she would send him back later in the day. He came back and we tested him, and he was positive for heroin. I told him that if he wasn't willing to stay on the campus and complete the detoxification, he should just go back home. He promised he would stay put and really participate in the program.

After two more escapes to use drugs and sleep at his mother's, he was terminated from the program. I advised his mother to love him enough to not allow him in her home unless he was clean from drugs. I don't know what happened to him, but if I had to guess, I would guess that he is in jail or prison, because he was on probation and was being randomly tested for drug abuse. My heart goes out to his mother, his son, and him. If we really want to help those we love, we must love them enough to do what is so hard for us to do.

It is so easy to enable those we love to hurt themselves and us. It is tough to face problems, and very tough to close people out of our lives to force them to face their addictions. Our intentions to help are often used as enabling by the one we want to help. I have learned that when I offer help and then my help is abused, I must withdraw any additional help. Sometimes it is really difficult to determine whether we are helping or enabling. And those individuals who are caught up in addiction are masters of manipulation.

Often, I find that people who come to our program asking for help, begging for an opportunity to change their life really only want a place to stay and food to eat. These people usually contribute the least, ask for the most and complain about everything. Still, I am willing to err on the side of enabling if I think I may provide help; however, once I recognize that my kindness is being taken for weakness I draw the line and give no more. Addiction is tough, it's complex, it destroys lives and it often kills. Those who are caught in it really do need help to break free because breaking free requires them to do a lot of work for themselves. For those of us who choose to help, we must learn all we can so we can determine what is helping, and what is enabling.

My advice to everyone who loves someone experiencing addictive, destructive behaviors is to help them physically, spiritually, emotionally, financially—all you can—but love them enough to let them go until they can and will accept help to change for good.

Often, family members are successful in getting their loved one who is experiencing addictions into a treatment program. Often, everyone feels relieved and wants to believe that the problem is solved. Most treatment programs are designed as intensive, 28 to 30 day live-in situations where no family members are permitted to contact the abuser, and only tobacco is permitted as an addiction.

Family members send their addicted loved one to treatment often believing that the program will fix the problem. More often than not, the problem isn't solved. Many clients don't actually backslide or relapse because they never really quit using. Many use in treatment, or as soon as they are released, or shortly after. The same is true when they are incarcerated or in hospitals. Many of these programs are very expensive and have beautiful facilities, and wonderful professional staff members. What happens? Why does abuse still occur in what looks like an environment that has been sanitized from access to addictive substances? Because those in power refuse to face the truth.

I've found that for treatment to be successful, the client first must really ___want___ to overcome the destructive lifestyle and addiction. Thirty days is seldom long enough. Usually the first 30 days in treatment, the client is in a state of chemical imbalance, physical discomfort, emotional pain, confusion and spiritual malnutrition. The first 30 days are best used to stop the insanity of drug use. These 30 days can be used to flip the switch to adjust from the enabling environment to another one that will not support abuse and to support the client physically, mentally, emotionally and spiritually. Those first 30 days are best used as a time for nurturing, for addressing the fact that the abuser has taken a first step in solving their problems. Many programs provide intensive counseling classes in subjects ranging from pharmacology to family systems to working through the disease concept by using the Twelve Steps during this period. Classes taken while an addict has just admitted to having a problem are not effective! In our program, we have found that intensive work has better results after the first 30 days of *just living* in a healing environment, not taking classes and trying to learn.

The most important aspect of any healing program is that the client has explored options and chooses a plan of action that feels right for him or her. Of course, if the client is limited in funds, the options are very few! The most important aspect for family members and/or friends choosing to help is that they take care of themselves and other family members. Addictions in a family environment injure everyone. Arizona Pathways honestly can't "fix" the addicted, but we can assist them in fixing themselves. One of the biggest obstacles to recovery from addictions is the guilt the addicted people experience when they recognize how much they have harmed others.

Taking care of yourself minimizes the negative effects of loving anyone struggling with addictions. Here is an example of a win-win situation where a mother, whose heart was hurt by her son who was abusing drugs, also was able to achieve healing.

Sam's mother called first, not Sam. She lived in another state and was researching options for her 44-year-old son who was addicted to cocaine. She was convinced that he needed a change of people, places and things. This mother, and the rest of her family, felt that they'd reached the end of their collective rope. Sam had lied, cheated and stolen from all of them. They had bailed him out of jail more than once and had paid for several 30-day treatment programs.

His mother said that sometimes Sam would work with his sponsor and attend Twelve Step meetings and stay clean and sober for a few months. I told her that if Sam was interested in the program at Arizona Pathways, he should call me directly. I also suggested that she attend Al-Anon meetings to help her understand how she had been enabling her son, causing stress to herself and her family. And, in the course of the conversation, I suggested that she find support through reading books and seeking support from her church and other groups.

Then Sam called. He said he really related to our philosophy about addiction so he booked a flight and joined our community. He fit right in and learned quickly. He became a role model for the other clients as he stayed in the program for one and a half years. His mother came to visit him when he was a resident, and she told me that she had found support for herself and the rest of her family. She had joined a church that was very much in alignment with the philosophy at Arizona Pathways.

When Sam got out, he chose to live in Arizona. He still keeps in touch with me, as does his mother. Her gratitude led her to send financial support to Arizona Pathways, and when I thank her after each donation she always says, "Thank you for giving my son back to me."

Chapter 5:

Twelve Steps and Arizona Pathways Steps

THE TWELVE STEPS OF ALCOHOLICS Anonymous have long been recognized as the primary effective approach for obtaining and maintaining sobriety. The Arizona Pathways program was successfully adapted to address addictive and destructive behaviors of all types. There seems to be a Twelve Step type of program for all kinds of human conditions from excessive gambling to shopping to overeating. The shared goal of Arizona Pathways' and all Twelve Step programs is to come to a spiritual awakening.

My understanding of the Twelve Step programs is based on reading most of their literature, attending Twelve Step meetings and fellowship events and working with clients experienced with the Twelve Step program.

Twelve Step programs are experienced through meetings, working with a sponsor, becoming a sponsor, providing service to others seeking help and social events. Twelve Step meetings are available all over the world. They are open to everyone desiring to stop drinking alcohol, using drugs, etc. Often judges, doctors, probation and parole officers, and managers of sober living programs require individuals to do "ninety and ninety," meaning attending 90 meetings in 90 days. During this period they are also required to select a sponsor. The sponsor serves as a mentor and guide through the Twelve Steps.

The meetings are usually referred to as either "speaker" meetings or "Big Book" studies. Those attending the meetings usually introduce themselves by saying, "My name is _____ and I am an alcoholic (addict, etc.)."

Everyone responds by saying, "Hi _____."

This format serves to welcome and include everyone in attendance, and also expresses the first step, breaking through the denial of the addiction experience. Often there is a celebration of those who have met goals of abstinence, 30 days, 90 days, etc., and token chips are given as acknowledgement. People usually share their stories of "using" and getting "sober" to inspire others.

Because Arizona Pathways follows some of the ideas of a Twelve Step program, here are the steps directly from Alcoholics Anonymous in italics and then my own understanding of their purpose.

Step 1: We admitted that we were powerless over our addictions, that our lives had become unmanageable. This first step has been interpreted to define addiction as a progressive incurable disease that can be fatal. Addiction affects sufferers three ways: mentally—by becoming obsessed with thoughts of using; physically—with compulsion to continue using regardless of the consequences and spiritually—by becoming totally self-centered.

Step 2: We came to believe that a Power greater than ourselves could restore us to sanity. This is generally agreed to mean that the spiritual principles of honesty, open-mindedness and willingness are required for healing to happen. It is spiritual work, not a religion, that allows us to create our own ideas about this power. In Twelve Step programs many turn to the group, the love that's encountered there, as the higher power, the "power of the group."

Response to Steps 1 and 2 by Arizona Pathways

I think that further definition is needed for Arizona Pathways' response to AA's Steps 1 and 2. Believing that the little words, "I am" are very powerful, we urge our clients to be very aware of the words that follow every "I am" statement. We encourage everyone to accept that they never can be less than a "child of God." We are all individual spiritual expressions of the Creator. We can never "be" less than that. When referring to addictions, we consider them to be a human experience, never a statement of "I am." Humans experience many things, including addictions. We can experience many feelings such as anger, happiness, sadness, etc. We can only "be" what we already are, and we are "of God." One of my favorite scriptures is 1 John 4:4: "Ye, are of God little children, and have overcome them because greater is he that is in you, than he that is in the world."

If a person goes to 90 meetings in 90 days and introduces herself in the manner, "My name is Jane and I am a child of God," I believe it will have a more positive effect than if that person refers to herself as an addict every day for 90 days.

In our work at Arizona Pathways, we admit that our human mind, personality, or ego of itself, is powerless over our addictions. It is truly a "dis-ease" that is experienced as obsession, compulsion, denial and spiritual void. Believing that all things are possible with Spirit, the concept of "incurable" is not recognized as truth. We also believe that the ultimate goal is spiritual awakening, and that honesty is a necessary spiritual principle to that awakening. While abstinence is the essential beginning, the only hope for recovery is profound emotional and spiritual change. Surrender (which is the feeling of "had enough," and "tired of fighting") must happen before change can happen. The addicted person must learn a new way to live by finding love and acceptance through fellowship.

Recognizing that we are greater than our humanness, that we are spiritual beings, leads to spiritual awakening. Guidance on our spiritual seeking journey comes from God through many sources: teachers, books, programs and experiences. We encourage our clients to be open-minded and find what works best to provide their individual needs, while also listening to the experiences of others in their midst.

We point out that any group, like Arizona Pathways, is not itself a higher power, but a sign that points to the higher power. We share the concept that the higher power – Spirit, God, Creator, Love, etc., is the one and only power that expresses in all things and all individuals. Programs, groups, fellowships, families, churches can create environments that express this presence in a powerful way.

Step 3: We made a decision to turn our will and our lives over to the care of God as we understood him. This step requires that a person move away from self will. Self-will is composed of such characteristics as closed mindedness, unwillingness, self-centeredness and outright defiance. The purpose of this step is to be willing to believe that faith of some kind--if only in the Twelve Step program--is possible. By recognizing that self will alone cannot save anyone from addiction to drugs or alcohol, the willingness to seek a higher power evolves. In the seeking comes the finding.

Response to Step 3 by Arizona Pathways

When it comes to turning our lives and will over to God, as we understand Him, at Arizona Pathways, our goal is to seek more understanding of God everyday. We look for experiences of God and talk about them together. We are not willing to turn our lives over to a stranger. For people who think in literal terms, God IS indeed considered a "stranger." Our program is all about empowering the individual to find the strength within (which is that God-source of strength) to start healing the wound that requests the addiction. We want to see self-empowerment. We do not want individuals to give their power over to some outside source such as the program or any staff member.

Step 4: We made a searching and fearless moral inventory of ourselves. This is often a turning point for many individuals, a time of deep personal reflection. This is a time to tell the truth, take stock of our assets and liabilities. A time to expose the lies we have told about ourselves, a time to separate fantasy from reality, to identify fear and how it works in our lives and how it is at the root of our addiction. Pursuing Step 4 allows us to chart a new course for our lives. It provides the initial insight we need to grow. It takes us from confusion to clarity, from resentment to forgiveness.

Response to Step 4 by Arizona Pathways

At Arizona Pathways we agree that deep personal reflection is necessary and our method is to do this gradually with prayer and meditation. As we seek to understand God and ourselves as the image and likeness of God, we also seek to see all the attributes of God (such as unconditional love, creativity, intelligence, skills, talents, and so on), and to recognize how failing to know ourselves as children of God has allowed us to live very destructive lives. We don't deny any of our past and our part in it. We change how we perceive ourselves and alter our role in the world we live in.

Step 5: We admitted to God, to ourselves and to another human being the exact nature of our wrongs. After completing the written inventory, it is essential to share it promptly. Recovery is built on spiritual principles such as surrender, honesty, trust, faith, willingness and courage. If we allow our feelings of shame and rejection to stop our progress, our problems will only be compounded. Through self-disclosure we feel connected with humanity perhaps for the first time in our lives. The person who listens to our Step 5 inventory should be someone who understands the process of recovery we are involved in and someone who is willing to help us through it. Such surgery of the spirit opens up old wounds, exposes carefully constructed lies, and tells us some painful truths. This process builds relationships with our sponsor, God and others.

Response to Step 5 by Arizona Pathways

There is a difference between "digging up bones" or focusing on character defects, and being willing to be in touch with our feelings and to let our feelings bring up past experiences that we are ready to review and learn from. We trust that our higher self (the child of God that we are) will know who to share these experiences with, when and how. Some individuals are best suited to assist with abuse issues, sexual issues, crimes, fears, failures, etc., than other individuals. We believe when you are ready, the perfect help is available. We have seen clients who are overwhelmed by pressure from a sponsor to complete the fifth step before they are ready, which can drive shame even deeper.

Step 6: We were entirely ready to have God remove all these defects of character. This is generally seen as a lifelong process, becoming ready to open our hearts and minds to the deep internal changes that can be brought about by the presence of a living God. Being able to see beyond our own interests and being concerned about the failings of others are striking changes considering that our raging self-obsession is at the core of our disease. We accept the responsibility for our behavior, good, bad or indifferent. The process involves practicing constructive behavior. The more attention we focus on our spiritual nature, the more it will unfold in our lives.

Response to Step 6 by Arizona Pathways

Spiritual awakening is indeed a lifelong process. As we learn our true identity as a "child of God," what are termed as "character defects" will be released and will fall away. We believe that God doesn't remove anything from us, but we must surrender and turn from what we no longer choose in our lives.

Step 7: We humbly asked him to remove our shortcomings: We ask our Higher Power for freedom from anything that limits our recovery. We ask for help because we cannot do it alone. We develop a relationship with our Higher Power through prayer. With knowledge comes freedom, freedom to choose. We sense that what is present throughout our search for spiritual growth is our ability to feel our Higher Power's love for us. God of our understanding has taken us from spiritually unconscious, hopeless addicts to spiritually aware recovering addicts eager to live.

Response to Step 7 by Arizona Pathways

We ask for and trust God to make us aware of any beliefs that limit our freedom to live and express as the children of God that we are. In this awareness we release any and all limitation, trusting in the love and power of God within to express in and through our lives. In this way we go from being spiritually unconscious human beings experiencing the dis-ease of addiction, to the spiritually aware children of God that we truly are, living in freedom.

Step 8: We made a list of all persons we had harmed and became willing to make amends to all. The objective is to clear away the damage we've done so that we can continue with our spiritual awakening, a process designed to free us from our past so we are able to live fully in the present. This causes us to let go of resentments and focus on our part in the conflicts in our lives, let go of expectations and blaming. We must be willing to do anything possible to repair the damage we have done, particularly by changing our behavior.

Response to Step 8 by Arizona Pathways

For some individuals, making a list is helpful; for others it is overwhelming. We trust as we become more and more aware of our true nature, that we will be guided spiritually on when and how and to whom to make amends. It is critical that we move from victim to victor, from victimizer to forgiven and from fear to faith. Changing our behavior to always doing the most loving thing we can in every situation will express our new understanding of our true nature and heal the pain of the past.

Step 9: We made direct amends to such people wherever possible, except when to do so would injure or harm others. The desire to make amends should be the primary motive for working the ninth step. We become aware of how we have changed as we make amends. We see how we are truly different, which enhances self-esteem.

Response to Step 9 by Arizona Pathways

We encourage everyone to follow this step by remaining prayerful and willing to right any wrong that they have caused to anyone else, following the spiritual guidance within, always asking, "is this the most loving action I can take?"

Step 10: We continued to take personal inventory and when we were wrong promptly admitted it. This step is commonly understood as a continuing self-examination, to become more aware of our emotions, our mental state and spiritual condition.

Response to Step 10 by Arizona Pathways

We prepare written answers daily to seven questions that make up our personal inventory and share our responses in group during Phase One of our residential program. Clients in Phases Two and Three write them and turn them in to staff. By sharing in group, clients have the opportunity to give and receive feedback from their peers and staff, allowing everyone to benefit. This is a process that helps develop the habit of using spiritual awareness.

Step 11: We sought through prayer and meditation to improve our conscious contact with God as we understood Him, praying only for knowledge of His will for us and the power to carry that out. We're powerless over our addiction, not that we won't be given the power to carry out the will of God of our understanding. At this point we are less motivated by pain and fear, driven more by our longing for continued recovery. There is no right way to pray and meditate. Prayer is talking to your Higher Power. Meditation is listening to your Higher Power.

Response to Step 11 by Arizona Pathways

We pray and meditate individually and as a group daily. We pray acknowledging the presence and power of God in all of our affairs and expressing our gratitude for the continuous flow of blessings, love and guidance.

Step 12: Having had a spiritual awakening as a result of these steps, we try to carry this message to addicts and alcoholics and to practice these principles in all our affairs. Using our spiritual principles to provide a stable environment to others strengthens our practice. It is time to be of service to the program and to other addicts in need.

Response to Step 12 by Arizona Pathways

Our program at Arizona Pathways also provides a stable, supportive environment for continued growth. Our clients become givers and receivers, no longer takers and users as they practice spiritual tools and experience life as spiritual beings having human experiences.

Twelve Step programs offer concise, linear and profound steps to healing from addiction. In our program we recognize their truth and respect them. Arizona Pathways doesn't specifically use the Twelve Steps, although the principles therein are present in the approach we do use. We have seen that the preliminary step of discovering our identity as spiritual beings, as children of God, is the hardest one. When that is understood and accepted, all the steps that follow tend to fall in place effortlessly. The shared goal of our program and Twelve Step programs is to come to a spiritual awakening. Some people find they can participate in both programs successfully, others find that they do better choosing one or the other.

Chapter 6:

The Five-Step Prayer

COMING TO KNOW ONE'S MIND, and then training one's mind to discontinue harmful belief patterns and embrace the truth, are both essential steps to happiness in all of the world's great spiritual traditions. For people working on overcoming addiction patterns, developing some skill in knowing and training one's own mind are critical to healing. Tools, such as meditation and practice dialogues are useful but the Five Step Prayer is the tool that we have found to be most consistently useful as a daily practice.

The Five-Step prayer is an informal version of a technique for praying that I learned through my study of Science of Mind. Ernest Holmes, the founder of Science of Mind, called this technique "Spiritual Mind Treatment." It is not only a wonderful, efficient method of prayer, it is a very efficient way of thinking in general. A Science of Mind slogan is "Change your thinking, change your life."

According to scripture, the Apostle Paul wrote to the Romans (in Romans 12:2) "Do not imitate the way of the world, but be transformed by the renewing of your minds, that you may discern what is that good and acceptable and perfect will of God." Most people who participate in our program are here because they desire a different quality of life. This prayer technique creates a renewing of the mind using five steps. Many of the people who have joined our community have spent time with the Twelve Step programs so they easily relate to the processes in the form of steps. The five steps of the prayer are, in order:

1. Recognition
2. Unification
3. Realization
4. Thanksgiving
5. Release

Let's take a look at each of the steps.

Recognition

In order for an addict to wake up and do the work of finding out what makes up their personality and soul, questions must be asked and answered. This is a series of questions and statements that all who are at Arizona Pathways use to recognize their understanding of God:

- How would you describe that reality you call God, spirit or your higher power?
- State in writing what you believe to be true about God.
- How would you describe God to someone who has never heard about God?

As an addict begins this exercise, it may surprise them how little or how much they believe they know about God. Maybe they have been uttering prayers to this stranger for years every time they became afraid or felt guilty. Or they may have felt completely alone and doubted the reality of a unifying God that connected them with all other people.

Here is how I describe God:

+ God is the intelligent, powerful Creator and maintainer of all life.
+ God is love and expresses that love through creation.
+ Because God loves what God creates, God provides abundantly for the fulfillment of every need.
+ God is all-powerful; there is nothing that God cannot do.
+ God is everywhere present.
+ There is no place where God is not.

The addict, or the person who loves an addict, may have ideas about God that are unique, or maybe his or her ideas were taught through a religion or by other people. Don't be afraid to challenge these ideas to see if you really believe them or if you've just accepted them because you've always heard them. Be willing to look for God and see how you would describe God for yourself.

Obviously, God is greater than our ability to know all there is to know about God. Most of us really don't know what we know or think to be true about God. We've never stopped to consider who or what God may be other than what we have heard, been told or experienced in some way. Yet the Twelve Step model suggests that we turn our lives over to a higher power, as we understand it. If our higher power is a stranger, that's a scary thought! Most churches and religions tell us to trust God, have faith in God, yet they fail to encourage us to seek and to know God personally. I found in my willingness to really work with the first step, *recognition*, my awareness and understanding continued to expand. I encourage you to be willing to be the same.

Unification

Here it is stated beyond doubt that the God described in your Recognition step is the One Life that expresses within all creation and us. If it is true that God is the one and only creator, is all-powerful and everywhere present, then it must also be true that God created me and you and everyone else and everything else. The life and lives that are expressed in this creation is one life, and it is God. So we are one with another, with God and with all of creation. God is love, and as I feel loved and loving, I am experiencing God's love expressing through me. There is no separation, there is one.

Realization

This step states the truth about a situation, one you are experiencing in some way, based on the *recognition* of God's presence and power and the *unity* of all, which then creates a different perception of what would at first seem to be a challenge. Here is a realization step, a prayer for freedom from alcoholism as an example from me to you:

> *God, as I am willing to experience the truth of my being—that I am a spiritual child of the Creator—I allow Your love to free me of the bondage of alcohol. God, you are all powerful. If you are the only power then there is no power in alcohol to interfere with my health, happiness or abundant supply. My real desire is to live in the constant awareness of Your love, Your power and Your presence. My belief about my desire for and my dependency on alcohol is based on the lie that I am less than you created me to be, which can never be true. My belief in the power of alcohol or in the possibility of an incurable disease is based on fear. Fear is about forgetting God. I choose to remember You as my source, as my power, as my supply. I know that with God, all things are possible.*

*I release myself from old, limiting beliefs and choose a life of
freedom from dependency on anything except God. I trust
in your constant guidance and protection as I choose to live
freely now.*

Can you see that prayer cannot come from the ego? When
prayer comes from your ego, it cannot work! The ego speaks to
the part of the person that is the person's own mind. When your
ego speaks to your own ego, is like praying to one's own self. But
when you use a heart that is open to the oneness of God to say
your prayer, the GOD part of you does listen!

Ego prays from fear. When an ego prays from fear, the prayer
is answered. The answer will be exactly what you fear.

Heart prays from love. When a heart prays from love, the
prayer is answered. The answer will be what you prayed for, or,
something even better.

Thanksgiving

These are statements that express gratitude for the answered
prayer. The thanksgiving step can only be expressed if the first
three steps have changed how you feel about the prayed for
situation. This means you have changed your feelings from fear to
faith. If you are still feeling concerned, it is important to go back
to the first three steps and work with them until you have a change
or a sense of freedom. Until you are praying from the heart and
not the ego. Here is an example of a prayer of thanksgiving:

*Thank you God for revealing the truth to me about my beliefs in
the power of alcoholism. I accept Your perfect healing in my mind
and in my life right now.*

Release

Finally, this is a statement that expresses a total and complete
acceptance of the solution, feeling free from concern:

As I release these thoughts and words, God, I know that I am free. I am Your beloved child and I know that You care for me, and so I let it be true. Amen.

Obviously, just writing and saying words is not going to cure anyone of alcoholism. The cure is in the changing of one's beliefs. It's about challenging fear based beliefs and replacing them with faith, with truth that eliminates fear. This is a process that continues throughout our human experiences. To be free, we must continually challenge beliefs and feelings that are based on our human, five sense-based perceptions. Again, practice makes perfect.

Most clients have great difficulty releasing their beliefs in the power of their drug or behavior of choice. After all, their lives have been in control of their beliefs and their power. To surrender those beliefs and to accept God as the only real power requires a sincere desire, a lot of courage, an open mind, honesty and perseverance.

Prayer versus fear

At Arizona Pathways, clients practice the five-step prayer here daily at the beginning of our group sessions, and learn to utilize it to pray for one another and for the Center as a whole. As we share the experiences of answered prayer, we begin to demonstrate to ourselves and others that it works. This, of course, encourages clients to trust in the process for their personal healing.

One of the greatest obstacles is fear. Jesus is said to have taught people to pray for believing. He taught that people had to believe in order to receive. So to pray for relief from whatever situation is bothering you, pray to believe that relief is possible. To really believe, we must find a way to connect our head to our heart.

Our human mind and ego perceives life objectively through

eyes, ears, nose, mouth and touch. Our human mind isn't capable of feeling emotion, and feelings and emotions are the language of the heart or of the spirit. Spirit speaks to us in feelings. Those feelings that we perceive as negative are simply the feelings that remind us that we are operating from our five senses and are not connecting with God.

When we see or hear something objectively and then become afraid, hurt or angry, these are emotions and feelings. They act as reminders that we are leaving out our awareness of God's presence and power. What you think of as a negative feeling is really God calling on you to pay attention. When we use our egos to feed on a negative situation, we make it worse by trying to control it with our mind. Here is an example of how fear prevents humans from avoiding the negative feelings that God sends as wake-up calls:

A man who was experiencing addiction came to Arizona Pathways for help, yet he was not yet ready to face the necessary opening of his heart. His fear compelled him to lie about several situations and even when he was called out on his lies, he was unwilling to go deep into his spirit because his ego kept reinforcing that he was a businessman. The fear of admitting his true self keeps him inside the cycle of drug abuse. He will need to reach a point where he can admit to his fear, drop his illusion of being a successful businessman and see that his fear is God's way of calling him to heal.

To build a connection between mind and heart we must always be aware of our spiritual reality and our oneness with our Creator. In this conscious awareness, we are at peace, are unafraid and are enthusiastic about life.

The practice of five-step prayer builds a very real connection between the person who prays it and the One who listens. Before you know it, your mind becomes trained to respond to life in this five-step sequence.

A look at choices, patterns, beliefs

When humans react to life from our human senses, the pattern is this: protect, defend, attack or seek revenge. When we respond to life from the awareness of ourselves as children of a God in whose presence and power we live, we now experience trust, love and forgiveness. Which do you prefer?

Society says, "Once an addict/alcoholic, always an addict/alcoholic."

My belief is, "Once a child of God, always a child of God.

Which belief do you choose? Which belief can you create? Which belief can you uncreate? Which theory supports freedom? Which theory supports the belief in a power other than God? In a power greater than God?

If you went to the doctor and he told you that you had an incurable disease, and that you would have to learn to manage the symptoms which would be very difficult, or you would die, how would you feel? If you went to another doctor and he told you that you had a disease that medicine couldn't cure but that God could, but you would have to be willing and ready to seek to know God, and to get in touch with your feelings so God could guide you so you could be healed, how would you feel?

Read the following two scenarios-in-one for an example of how treatment for addiction might occur:

+ You know you have an illness.
+ You go to a doctor.
+ He tells you that your disease is incurable.
+ He says that managing your symptoms will be difficult.

+ He tells you that if you do not manage your symptoms, you will die.
+ How do you feel? What do you do? Think about it. Do you get upset with the doctor? Do you get upset with yourself? Do you resolve to manage your symptoms to the best of your ability? Or do you resolve to let nature take its course and you prepare to die?
+ Let's say you decide to go to another doctor for a second opinion.
+ You now know you have an illness that is very serious.
+ This second doctor is quite different from the first doctor.
+ This doctor tells you it is true that there is no pill to cure you, but there is hope.
+ She tells you chemistry will not cure you, but God will.
+ She says you must first be willing and ready to seek and know God.
+ She tells you that you must get in touch with the feelings in your heart.
+ She smiles and says that God will guide you through your feelings.
+ Finally she says that following your feelings will lead you to help in healing.

Now how do you feel?

The fact is that addiction is becoming more and more widespread and is destroying more lives every day. Our society believes that addiction is:

+ an incurable disease

+ that probably most victims of it are genetically predisposed to it
+ investing in research and treatment is worthless
+ a need to punish those who cannot keep their symptoms in remission by sending them to jails and mental hospitals
+ to be medicated for relief

Society is afraid and continues to use fear-based attempts to solve this challenge.

Most of the addicted people I've met are more than intelligent enough to understand that to change their beliefs is to change their lives. But it takes more than an intellectual understanding of this truth to actually manifest that change—it takes practice.

With practice, the brain's actual connections—those same connections that previously were trained by substance abuse and all the circumstances that preceded it—begin to actually change, to develop new pathways. Like anything that we become proficient at in our lives, practice is the key to achieving this goal. The five-step prayer is certainly not the only tool that can be practiced to train our unruly minds, but it is a beautiful, creative, comforting and effective one that can be used throughout a lifetime.

Chapter 7:

The Power of Community

MOST PEOPLE CAUGHT IN THE traps of various addictions feel alone, unworthy, guilty, ashamed, unforgivable and greatly afraid. They usually are like birds of a feather and they tend to flock together and hang out with others in similar situations. This flocking behavior also causes them to feel stuck, hopeless and depressed. Continued substance abuse is the only sure thing— the temporary ease of pain and the only answer of which they are sure.

The first time our clients at Arizona Pathways hear "you are a child of God and you are loved," they are usually surprised at how foreign, yet how good, those words sound. They start hoping that the statement is true. When others treat them as though it is true, they begin to believe it and feel it. Finally, they begin to experience the "natural high" of knowing who and what they really are through learning to treat others the way they enjoy being treated. It takes time until they can except that they are lovable and that they are really loved. Once this happens, they begin to find that accepting others and caring about them is easy and natural. This is the healing power of community.

I often notice how separate people can become. Neighbors often don't know their neighbors, or even their names. Houses are fenced off from one another. People come home from work, open the garage door with their remote opener and go inside. Often they barely know their family members or housemates. They go to their own room or space, turn on music, computers, video games or talk or text on their cell phones. It might be shocking to know how little conversation, touching and sharing is happening in homes today. Everyone is busy and connected to something electronic so they are alone no matter who is around. Technology is great but it often replaces human contact and intimacy. I find this concerning because people need to belong and feel accepted.

Sometimes when natural disasters happen, people put aside what was important just before the crisis and rush to help each other. I remember when I was younger and lived in Michigan, which has really tough ice and snow conditions in winter. We lived in the country on a dirt road. Every winter the snow would drift across our road so deep that no one could get out. The neighborhood men would dig out a tractor and contact everyone in our area to see what they needed. Then they would take the tractor in the blizzard to town to get groceries and medicine for everyone. Sometimes some of us would run out of heating fuel or the water lines would freeze up. When this happened, the tractor would come and take us to someone's home in the neighborhood until the storm broke and the county snowplows could clear the road. Those were cold and miserable days, but I have fond memories of how everyone took care of each other.

At Arizona Pathways, we take care of each other in that way. Several clients have had operations and painful medical treatments. Some have experienced AIDs or cancer. The members of our community take care of and help those who need help. They share their clothes and personal items like razors, toilet paper, soap and towels. Everyone here knows that they are God's beloved offspring and they know that this is the truth about themselves and everyone else. This is the common bond that joins us to each other.

No, everyone doesn't always get along with everyone else in our treatment center, and this is true at any center. There are personality clashes. People come here not knowing who they are as God's children. They have experienced abuse so their identity is that of a victim. Believing this is true, they perceive everything as being done *to* them.

I have come to believe that everyone, every single living person, has experienced what he or she has perceived as abuse. In some families violence, rage, anger, sexual abuse and neglect are so prevalent that it "seems" normal. (Check www.acestudy.org to see how Adverse Childhood Experiences—ACEs—are categorized and rated.) To others any exposure, no matter how minor, to violence or personal violation is experienced as traumatic. It is all relative to an individual's perception of what is normal. It is how people respond to these traumatic experiences that determine the long-term effects.

Many clients have chosen to experience their personal traumas as an excuse to become addicted to destructive lifestyles. They continue to be victimized over and over. They continue to choose people and environments that will continue the pattern of abuse. They are unwilling to forgive their victimizers and are unwilling to accept any responsibility for continuing to put themselves in vulnerable situations. They talk about their past abuse all of the time to anybody who will listen. They cannot change because they are unwilling to change their thinking. Abuse has become what their whole life is about and they use it for an excuse to not accept responsibility for their current or future experiences.

Others have been willing to draw strength from past abuses. They draw strength from the fact that they have survived. They learn to see what they can change in their thinking about the past, about the abusers and about themselves. They seek their inner spiritual power to stop the cycle of abuse and to set themselves free.

We reaffirm over and over that no one is what they have experienced, or what they have done, or what has been done to them. They are of God and are here to express God in the unique way that only each one of us can. Conflicts provide opportunities to learn and practice positive techniques of conflict resolution. Being a part of something good, something positive, is what causes people to help others and to feel comfortable asking for and receiving help from others.

We all know how good it feels to make a positive impact on the lives of others. At Arizona Pathways we help people to become aware that by accepting help from others we provide an opportunity for the giver to feel good by helping others. Pride often prevents us from living in the positive energy of the flow of giving and receiving. Those living in chemical addictions have usually become takers, not receivers. Takers never have much to give because they take from others and give everything to their addictions. Being a taker creates guilt and shame, and a mental attitude of lack and limitation. For this reason most successful recovery programs require service work in the community, volunteer work. Living free requires learning to live as a part of or member of humanity, knowing that giving is as necessary as receiving.

Community is a strong influence in the success of our clients. Community support encourages people to continue in the program for a long enough period of time to find freedom from the addictions to destructive behaviors. It takes months of abstinence, nutrition, rest and emotional and spiritual support for the brain chemistry to normalize.

The average time of residence in our program is one year.

Many stay longer—all of our staff members are former clients in the program. Often people will leave after 30 to 90 days. Most of these individuals return later and start over. Usually they realize that it takes time to get physically healthy, to gain mental clarity about their personal thoughts and beliefs about addictions, relationships and spirituality. Freedom from addictions requires a changing or renewing of the mind, a release from the limited self-identity to accepting the broader view of themselves as spiritual beings with human experiences.

I like the quote about spiritual beings and would like to hear it more often: *We are not human beings having a spiritual experience; we are spiritual beings having a human experience.* The origin of the phrase may have been Pierre Teilhard de Chardin who said, "*We are not human beings on a spiritual journey. We are spiritual beings on a human journey.*" Author Stephen Covey used the quote in his book, published in 2000, *Living the 7 Habits: Stories of Courage and Inspiration.* You may have heard it in a presentation from Dr. Wayne Dyer. Then, they learn to understand that the past cannot be changed, but their perceptions relating to the past can. They can learn to see things from a broader awareness. Lessons can be learned from past experiences to help break addictive and obsessive behaviors. Changing the minds and habitual behaviors is a process and takes practice.

It is the work that addicts must learn to take on and do one day at a time. Being in the now, that is taking the moment for what it, knowing that you have the power to change anything at any time is key. The time is always now. The place is always here. The advent of how quantum physics plays a role in human behavior is about to become more widely known and accepted. As someone who has worked in rehabilitation of human spirits for so many years, I look forward to staying abreast of this scientific knowledge as it will combine with what is now typically considered spiritual knowledge and applying what I learn to improve the services offered at Arizona Pathways.

A community working together to practice these changes is necessary for success in learning to live in positive and healthy lifestyles. The community provides an environment that encourages people to fix themselves. A community, to work well, requires individuals to be self-responsible. We can share tools, techniques and opportunities so each person can find his own answers, his own pathway. As clients create relationships within the community of the treatment center and beyond, they support the spiritual paths of each other. In accepting responsibilities as a community member they discover and strengthen their individual talents and skills and the whole community benefits. The members of this community are responsible for maintenance, cooking, cleaning, landscaping, clerical work, providing music, mentoring and whatever else they have skills and talents to offer. This creates mutual respect and appreciation for everything provided.

At Arizona Pathways we teach our own specific brand of spiritual tools to help in the process of "renewing the mind," which is a statement found in the Bible, to experience life in a new healthy, peaceful and productive way. The community environment of a treatment center like Arizona Pathways is the perfect place to practice and become skillful in the use of these tools.

Chapter 8:
Spiritual Tools

EVERYONE HAS INSIDE OF THEM all the tools they need for knowing that they are a spiritual beings. They also have tools to prove that actions speak louder than words. So, when a spiritual being is confronted with a difficult situation, they can use action as a tool to create an experience in which learning and healing become possible.

Written Dialog

We all have conversations within our own mind with different aspects of ourselves. Everyone has a Wise Mind, or the mind of spirit within and everyone has one or more voices expressing ego identity. The exercise of writing these inner conversations causes us to recognize our beliefs and to understand from where they originated.

In the following example of an interior dialogue W represents the Wise, or spiritual mind, and E represents the human ego.

W: *I choose to be free from addictive and destructive habits from this day forward.*

E: *Right. After years of abusing drugs and alcohol, now, you're just going to choose to stop?*

W: *Yes, I know it might not be easy so I'm willing to ask* *for help from others. I also know that I must pray and meditate.*

E: *How many times have you said you were done, finished, only to pick it up again and again?*

W: *You're right. I thought I could just say "no." I also thought that finding the right relationship would be the answer. I also thought that money to buy cars, clothes, jewelry, houses and vacations would be enough.*

E: *See, nothing works. You have tried it all—religion, love, possessions, Twelve Step programs, prescribed replacement drugs, psychotropic drugs, etc. and it all seems to work for awhile. But, you lose it all and go right back to the addictions. You'll never get free.*

W: *You just said the secret word, "free." Before it was all about abstinence, counting days, talking about using or not using, which is always talking about using. Always talking about being an addict. This isn't free, it's miserable. So after awhile I just give up.*

E: *So now what are you doing to be free? Free from what?*

W: *Now, I'm talking about freedom from the desire to use, freedom to feel. I now understand that addiction is a human experience, one that I am tired of and don't want to continue with. I now know that I am a child of God. I was created by God to express God as only I can. This understanding is what allows me to experience freedom.*

E: *It sounds interesting but do you really think you can do this? After all those failures to stay clean and sober?*

W: *I know I can. I mean I know we can. I need your help and support. Will you agree to be that spiritual, beloved child of God with me?*

E: *I don't know if it will work, but I'll do my best.*

W: *Good. The part about doing your best works because God does the rest. When you say, "I don't know if it will work," you are saying that you still have some doubt. What can I do to get you to stop doubting?*

E: *I think I can replace my doubt with realization. I realize that I no longer need to doubt when I know God.*

W: *Thanks. Of ourselves we do nothing. It is the spirit God within that is doing the hard part. We are free and we can always be.*

The idea is never to attempt to destroy ego, but to resolve inner conflicts caused by erroneous beliefs based on prior experiences. The goal is to integrate ego with spirituality. To this "one mind" all things are possible. The goal is also to create awareness within individuals relating to how they choose to act, believe and feel. Instead of giving power over to drugs, drink or behaviors that deaden emotions, belief that with trust in God and willingness to bring them up and deal with them, painful emotions related to memories can heal and stop the need for numbing them.

The act of writing is powerful. Written dialogue brings clarity to how you got to where you are, and allows you to consciously change your mind and to change your life.

Once a person becomes skilled in using this tool, written dialogue really helps to find the God-given wisdom within. For clients at Arizona Pathways who do not like to write or think they are bad at writing, we tell them that writing helps them to tell the truth to themselves. It is difficult to lie in writing! Every individual knows what is right and best, but they need to find a way to connect with that wise spiritual being within and to clear away the lies and fears of human ego. As children of the creator we always have God's wisdom, intelligence and power and love available. There is such great value in writing. First, in those who resist it, when it does get written, there is a feeling of accomplishment. Second, it is indeed therapeutic. It is a gateway for emotions to spill out, to be loosed from the cage of the soul. And third, it serves as a record of the progress of healing.

You may find yourself questioning my statement that we all know what's right and best for ourselves. It certainly appears, in our human experience, that this is not true. But be honest with yourself. Think of all the times that you have done something that proved to be wrong. You knew that you had a notion that it was wrong—you just didn't pay attention to it. You chose to disregard it.

I know personally when I have something that I want to do in my humanness, something that I want to happen, and I have something within me that causes me to be uncomfortable with my decision, rather than honor that knowing what is right and best, I often find I go out and seek other people to get them to support and validate my human perception of what is right and best. If I can find others to validate what I want from my ego point of view I think I don't have to listen and be guided by that spiritual, wise voice that's coming from within. Every time I have done that, I have to say that I've regretted it.

I do believe that each one of us has an inner knowing, an intuition or, you may call it conscience, and we do have it. We may drown it out with other people's voices and support; we may have drowned it out with alcohol and/or drugs. We may find many reasons not to listen or to not feel it. But to find freedom, it is important to be willing to honor that knowing, that wise being that we are, that spiritual being, that image and likeness of our creator that does know, that does love, that is wise and powerful and intelligent. When we honor that awareness we do make the right and best choices. The other component of this is that it takes time to go inside and question yourself, your motivation, and it takes patience to listen for that true voice. *nowhere* in human existence is this taught, unless someone has a grandmother or parent or teacher or friend who knows it and cares enough to have the patience to talk about it and to teach it and to *give it permission.*

When writing a dialogue, it is best to continue working on it until you can feel the validation that releases fear and feel secure that you are doing the right thing. Our clients use this tool to resolve all the issues that have come up for them when struggling with whether to use or not to use; whether to stay or whether to run, whether to cry or to stuff their feelings. The written dialogue provides that strength in knowing what is really true, what is really right.

The tool of written dialogue is very helpful in the process of renewing minds. At Arizona Pathways, together we learn that when a client admits to craving their drug of choice, we know they are close to a relapse unless we can get them to talk about what they are really feeling. Usually the craving for a drug of choice means they are feeling angry or fearful. Naming these emotions as "a craving" creates a set up for a relapse.

The truth of these situations is really, "I don't like how I feel." Relapse is choosing to use a chemical or behavior to block out these feelings. A much better option is to be willing to discover why you feel the way you feel. The following is a version of a written dialogue that works to tap into your feeling:

Situation: My friend has said something cruel to me and my feelings are hurt.

Step one: *I must ask, "What is happening here?" My ego says, "She was so mean me and I do not deserve that!"*

Step two: *Now assess my ego. "Based on my prior experience with her, I understand why I feel hurt by her actions."*

Step three: *Ask, "I wonder what this really means? Maybe this isn't about me. Maybe she is having a bad day."*

Step three: *Listen or watch for an answer. Be patient. Know that I will be shown!*

Step four: *See what shows up and then realize that I can forgive her and know that what she needs is love.*

At this point you are beginning to understand that the world is not about you. Now the answer comes from your higher mind and it causes you to see clearly and to recognize that you cannot be a victim and that someone or some situation is asking for love.

Step five: *Now I can ask, "What is the most loving thing I can do in this situation?" This response is always clear, calm and inspiring.*

Seven Questions

Self-awareness is key to reforming addictive behavior. There is a tool for learning how to be self-aware and we use it in our facility. Telling the truth is the foundation to finding freedom from addictions. Group therapy sessions are very effective utilizing this process. Each client is asked to journal the answers to seven simple questions every evening before they retire. Here are the questions:

+ What did I learn about myself today?
+ What was I afraid of today?
+ What was I dishonest about?
+ What was I angry about?

83

- What am I thankful for?
- How did I experience God today?
- What do I plan to do with my new day when I awake?

These are rather simple questions, but they are also very complex questions. They serve the purpose of helping people to empty their stress so they can relax and rest and sleep well. They also serve the purpose by sharing them in group to have other people become aware of how we're being dishonest, how we're people-pleasing, how we're just saying the same thing day after day, how we happen to write answers that seem to be what we want other people to hear. When clients actually express that gut-wrenching, tear-jerking truth, that's the beginning of their freedom.

Freedom happens when you understand addiction is natural.

Freedom happens when you realize that you bought into the false belief that addiction to chemicals or destructive behaviors will fulfill your cravings.

Freedom happens when you realize that only spiritual knowledge and understanding will fill all of your needs.

Overcoming addiction is a continual process to be embraced and even enjoyed in terms of the work individuals must do to keep gaining wisdom and understanding.

In our daily group session, each person has the opportunity to share his or her answers to these questions. Even if they choose not to share with the group, they always share with themselves. We recognize that internal dialogue just as important as group dialogue. We encourage them to talk with a counselor one-on-one as well.

Meditation

Another important tool that we practice every morning at Arizona Pathways is group meditation. There are several types of meditation that we practice so that clients learn what works best for themselves. It is with meditation that we watch and get to know our minds and to experience the presence of the spirit that resides there.

The first kind we learn is silent meditation. This involves 15 minutes of sitting in the quiet with an attitude of relaxing our bodies and just being in the quiet place of listening to the spirit within.

Guided visualization is another very popular form of meditation, using recordings or creating our own. Guided visualization activates that part of the mind that dreams and/ or imagines. Guided visualizations can direct the subconscious mind to reveal to us things that we might want to know about ourselves; what our fears are, what might be the cause of certain illnesses or other concerns.

We also do meditations that are just sitting and focusing, as on the flame of a candle, on a sound or on counting breaths.

We also do meditations that are directed specifically to help relax the physical bodies by tensing up certain muscles then relaxing them. This helps people who are stressed and feel uptight. This is a good form of meditation to use in the beginning of learning to meditate because many people have difficulty just being still and allowing their body to be quiet.

We might start and end a meditation practice with the universal sound of "om." All forms of meditation are beneficial and everyone finds their favorites.

Group meditation brings a powerful sense of unity and a connecting energy that is very healing.

My other favorite meditation is just the stillness, being alone and quiet. I like to use this form of meditation in connection with journaling or writing. One of the favorite meditations is to be still and quiet for 15 to 20 minutes, just listening, and then to pick up a pad and pen and begin to write. Sometimes clients have wonderful clarity about answers to questions or get a sense of direction to follow.

There is no right or wrong way to meditate. Meditation is something that is not a cult activity. It is simply a time to honor self and to honor God. It is setting aside the time and space to focus on spiritual healing or strengthening in whatever form we happen to be using at the time.

One of the tools that I have learned in meditation is to set clearly in my mind an intention to be still. A good way to meditate is to take a deep breath, and say, "I will be still." Continue to repeat this mantra until you are still.

Another word of advice is to also tell yourself in this quietness that whatever sounds you might hear during this time will simply remind you to be still. This is really helpful if you're in a place where someone might open the door or the phone might ring or when someone who doesn't know that you're taking this time for meditation might interrupt you in some way. Or if you are outdoors and there are birds, wind, airplane sounds, etc. Just that silent command to yourself, "I will be still, and that every sound that I hear simply reminds me to be still" is very helpful and supportive.

Meditation is a gift. It is one of the greatest gifts we can give ourselves. It is actually dedicating time and space to allow God to speak to us, to allow us to actually hear not from our ego, not from other people, but actually to hear the truth. Meditation really allows us to release our fears and to get clarity. It becomes a cherished time.

It's interesting that it also is one of the tools that we find the most resistance to. Of all the clients that we work with at Arizona Pathways, we find that the willingness to be still is where we find the greatest resistance. There are a lot of beliefs that people with substance abuse or other addictive behaviors have that they cannot be still; a belief that they cannot meditate.

It's amazing how powerful the ego shows itself when someone is asked to learn to meditate. And one of our theories is that what we resist the most is really what is probably what is best for us. So we keep practicing and we encourage people to know and believe that meditation does take practice. It takes a commitment. It takes a willingness. It is all about overcoming resistance.

Our ego certainly doesn't want us to know how to do it because it is one of the most healing tools, the most healing opportunities; the most healing gifts that has ever been given to man. The ego doesn't like meditation because it likes to feel in control at all times. Meditation takes away some control from the ego. Meditation is practiced all over the world. It's Biblical, it's catholic; it's part of every religion in some form. It is not always called meditation, but there is always that thing called silent prayer or repeating a verse or performing a ritual. All these are forms of meditation. Meditation can also be an action. There can be movement that is meditative as in Tai Chi. There can be exercise that is meditative such as yoga. So there is no particular rule on how you meditate. The great idea of allowing ourselves that time and that space, honoring that life that we are, and allowing it to be healed and allowing it to be guided and directed is one of the most powerful gifts that we can give ourselves and to encourage others to accept for themselves.

Being at Arizona Pathways

Here is how we use the spiritual tools I've described in the program at Arizona Pathways. We use the five-step prayer process by writing prayers daily and sharing them with each other. We have group classes in the afternoons that focus on teaching the process of the prayer, written dialogue and meditation. The journaling, the seven questions that everyone answers and shares helps clients to become more honest, and to realize what they have in common. The sharing time helps to heal the fear, guilt and shame.

We are also blessed with spiritual counselors who teach spiritual principles like forgiveness and unconditional love. Twice a week, a local naturopathic college, Southwest College of Naturopathic Medicine & Health Sciences, offers a holistic, natural medicine clinic for our clients that include acupuncture and nutrition. We have a Sunday celebration service in which our clients actively participate. A licensed substance abuse counselor meets with clients for both group and individual counseling. Sometimes, when finances permit, we provide our clients with membership at the YMCA.

Clients are responsible for their living area, which is checked and monitored for cleanliness, safety and banned substances. If they don't know how to make a bed or clean a floor, they are taught. They also share responsibility for yard work and clean up of the property. Everyone is assigned chores to contribute to the common good.

The environment is home-like rather than institutional. Clients are not told the rules then kicked out if they break them. Instead they experience how it is. There are rules and consequences, but we pay attention to each client's response to them so they can understand themselves better and change destructive behavior. When infractions occur, they are dealt with on an individual basis. As a mother of two sons, I know that one size doesn't fit all and that every situation is different, with new opportunities to learn and grow.

Clients have differences of opinion. We allow for conflict, and we work together for resolution as an opportunity for self-understanding. We do not allow violence or threats of violence, but we do allow people to disagree, expressing their opinion and allowing others to express theirs. We practice using the spiritual tools described earlier in resolving issues of relationships, money management, careers and personal interaction with others.

We teach life skills as needed, working with clients to learn how to manage their money, to budget, to become financially responsible. When a client is ready to go to work, we assist them with resume writing, learning how to find the good in themselves and expressing it outward as far as relating to employment, or helping them find a particular training or vocational school. When they go back to work, one of the things we require them to do for the first month is to bring their paychecks back to the Center. Our financial person assists them in being responsible for their program fees and to budget their money to take care of whatever their other financial responsibilities they have. This allows them to continue to mature as responsible adults and to feel better about themselves because now they can respect what they are doing.

Some people aren't ready to do this, and that simply is an announcement that they are not yet willing to be responsible. Sometimes they feel the urge to give that money to the provider of their drug of choice, to return to the addictive behavior. So we've found that working together to be honest about how much money they're earning and where it's going is helpful in assisting them to bring awareness to their behavior, and to become someone that they like and someone that they respect.

We have relationships with temporary employment agencies and permanent employers who are aware of our work, knowing that our clients are working to become free from addictions, and will hire them. We find that the more open we are about someone's background and why they're at Arizona Pathways, the more open employers are. Clients, some of them who have felony convictions or have done prison time, might have believed they were not employable, that if they tell the truth they will not be accepted. They learn to overcome those erroneous beliefs by developing those relationships with employers that are open to accepting them for their skills, their intelligence, their willingness to work. The program is about helping people learn to live as children of God, not as felons, not as ex-cons, not as addicts and alcoholics, but as truly gifted, skillful, lovable and intelligent individuals.

A holistic approach is essential for anyone choosing to live life free from bondage to something they've given power to. Our program is simple yet comprehensive, and spiritually based. It is based on the perception that we are spiritual beings, children of the Creator, and that in addiction, we are getting lost in a very human experience. By understanding that addiction is natural, we find that the addictive behaviors can be the path that leads us back to the truth of who and what we are.

Success at Arizona Pathways

When asked by clients, potential clients or just people in general how successful our program is, my reply is always, "What is it you mean by success? What are you measuring?" Success in traditional treatment usually means how many days, months, years of sobriety.

Success is something quite different to me. Success to me is that someone's life is better. They have more hope. They have more opportunities. They are willing to experience life without abusing chemicals. According to this definition of success, we are 100 percent successful.

Every person who has come to Arizona Pathways, whether for one day, (which is very unusual), or off and on for several years, (which is more common), improves their life. They have more potential to be an asset to society. They have more potential to contribute to the good of all.

Abstinence means that someone is not doing, eating or drinking or using something that they desire to use, drink, eat, or do. So abstinence is a state of deprivation. Abstinence is a state of denying ourselves what we believe we want. That's the reason I don't feel that the practice of abstinence means success. I believe success is being free from desiring anything that would cause damage to ourselves or to anyone else or to the society we live in. That is my personal definition of successful living.

My goal is to free clients from destructive behavior. What this looks like is different for everyone.

Imagine that someone has gone through the program, loved it, did the work, got back into society. Then they are at a party where an opportunity to drink comes up---do they do it just for the fun of it, thinking, "this time it will be for fun, not because I feel hurt and want to be numb?" This is a common situation. But it provides a new opportunity to learn.

Ideally, after being at Arizona Pathways, clients will start their own program of Loyalty To Self where, in the above situation they say, "I totally quit drinking to heal the pain I felt in childhood and I've been clean for 12 years and here I am at this party and it's available to me again but this time in a fun way and yeah, it might be great to drink again but darn it, I did all that work and I know that having a beer will take me back so I am going to just skip it and go over there and talk to Joe instead."

Some people actually learn that they can become social users of the substance that took them into self-destruction. Some must learn that they can never use it again in order to be free.

The long-term goal of Arizona Pathways program is for people to become successful in living, and living in a sense of being free to fulfill their life's purpose.

People get upset when people that have a history of substance abuse get a little clean and sober time, and then they go back and indulge themselves again. Many people call this relapse. Relapse, to me, is something that happens many times for most people involved in the process they call recovery. Very few people, although I know some, decide that they are going to abstain from abusing their chemical or behavior of choice and from that point on, stay in that abstinence. And to those few that stay in that abstinence, one of two things happen. They either become very, very miserable and they substitute. If it's a substance they then substitute one substance for another. If it is a behavior then they substitute another destructive behavior. Any excess is destructive.

A common medical model actually supports prescribing replacement drugs. Some individuals substitute a behavior in an attempt to replace the desire for their chemical or behavior of choice, For instance, if someone is an alcoholic, they may abstain from drinking, but they may become a sex addict or rageaholic, shopaholic, or they may become addicted to gambling or developing an eating disorder. Abstinence often results in an exchange of one addiction for another.

Being aware of this, our goal is not to focus so much on abstinence, but to focus on the truth of what and who each one of us really is, what the truth about what addiction is, and the truth about why they're here. As we focus of getting to the truth of things, someone can lose their desire. Instead of being in abstinence, still having the desire of wanting that which they know is not good for them, they can lose the desire. They then no longer are tormented. They no longer are struggling. They are no longer switching one desire for a substitute. They simply no longer want that which is not good for them. To me, that is success. That is the goal. Loyalty To Self.

The truth is anyone can choose to use drugs or alcohol anywhere at any time. This is always an option. Hopefully those who have made it all the way through the program and maintained their sobriety and have learned to use the tools that we share and believed the truth of what they really are, for them there will be no *desire* to make the choice to abuse substances or destructive behaviors again. That is the goal, to lose the desire, to move beyond the desire and change their desire to the desire to be free. The best way to change the object of our desires is to change our mind about who and what we really are. In my mind I believe that everyone is an individual and unique expression of a spiritual creator and that this creator is all-powerful, everywhere present and unconditionally loving.

When were are talking about clients who have been in bondage to chemicals and/or other destructive behaviors for 20, 30 years or more, why shouldn't it take three, four, five, or more years to find freedom? When the private, or government insurance companies are only willing to fund short-term treatments (often only outpatient), most people have no resources to provide for the length and/or quality of help that really helps them. The same funding sources also usually do not allow alternative types of treatments under the illusion that one size fits all. We all know this is never true with members of the human race. The only long term solution the "system" provides and funds is prison, where drug use is rampant.

Overcoming obstacles to freedom

Substance abuse happens in both the mental body and the physical body, and obstacles to choosing freedom from them happen in those bodies as well. Here are some observations about why it takes so long to find freedom in the physical sense as well as the spiritual sense.

One of the main obstacles is what I call the "fence sitter" mindset. A fence sitter is someone who appears to be unwilling or unable to make a choice between positive change and remaining the same. Many people resist change, even the chance to make a choice to change for the better.

It's important to explore conflicting beliefs, relating to any situations one wants to change. But as long one holds conflicting beliefs, real change is impossible. For instance, when clients believe "once an addict/alcoholic, always an addict/alcoholic" freedom from addictions can't be experienced.

A fence sitter desires a new life yet is afraid to let go of the old lifestyles. Fence sitters want to believe that they're a child of God and that God loves and cares for them and is present and powerful in their life, yet they are afraid to let go of that familiar, good feeling that the chemical abuse or behavior abuse has provided them. It's exactly that place of being afraid, unable to go without anything as you let go of one belief to embrace something else.

You can't do positive thinking if you can't release your negativity.

Fence sitting is miserable and depressing. Fence sitters can't go anywhere because they can't decide which way to go. Fence sitters are stuck, leaning one way then the other way. This is where many find themselves stuck for a long time. Eventually, if they don't take a chance and choose a new way, they fall back into the familiar old way.

The only time we ask clients to leave is when we see them leaning more and more towards the old, less and less willing to practice the skills, the tools that they need for a new life.

Sometimes we must give them a gentle nudge and push them over to the side that they are leaning toward. This means that if they are leaning to "no change" we push them to make sure that they wallow in no change for a while until they get tired of it, reach the lowest of the low so that they can climb back to "change." We make sure that those who are asked to leave always know that if they choose to come all the way over to the other side of the fence, they are welcome, but no more fence sitting and no more leaning one way or the other. It is a difficult choice that everyone must make.

The point is that even if they lean to and fall off the fence on the "I choose no change" side, we still love them. Some have said, "I've never been told before, while being kicked out of a program, that I am loved!"

The Arizona Pathways program empowers people to see choice, this fence, and what it looks like on either side. If they fall off the fence on the side of "no change" there are good things such as the temporary relief substance abuse offers. And, there are bad things—substance abuse is destructive—but if a client chooses to change there will be only good in working to stop their own destructive behavior.

This is a choice that separates abstinence from freedom. Abstinence is a kind of fence sitting. Freedom is walking away from the belief in and the desire to perform destructive behaviors. Freedom is experienced by making a choice. Sitting on the fence is risking that fall. When someone falls, sometimes they die. It is choosing a path of lightness, a path of love, a path leading away from fear and bondage. For broken people who do not have a concept of what "a path of lightness, a path of love" is, we use pets and nature to teach these concepts.

One of the clients who seemed to have great difficulty in choosing, who was always interested in new ways, always interested in spiritual principles, always interested in loving everyone except himself used to say "I just don't understand why I can't get it right, just can't be free." I told him that it was like he was walking around with his arms full of garbage. God was trying to hand him flowers, and he wouldn't put down the garbage. He wasn't putting down what was stinking up his life so he couldn't accept the freedom that was being offered to him.

This seems to be the grave challenge for people desiring to make major changes in their lives, not just people with substance abuse problems. When we feel that sense of being unsettled, not being able to go forward in life, not wanting to go backward, not wanting to stay the same, we are in that place where we have to make a choice.

How do you take the fear out of making a choice?

You write about what happens on each side of the fence for you, then you remove the fear from each side! If you fall off the fence on the side of "I choose to live the status quo of drug use, self destruction, unhappiness" then I cannot fear the consequences. This lack of fear of consequence will help you accept whatever happens in that choice—either hitting the skids, death, or getting woken up to some other choice by what seems to be an accident. If someone chooses to change, to get help, to work hard to create the change, to build in some time for healing, some time for self (in order to face pain, heal it, wear the scar of it but learn not to pay much attention to that scar, and live in a way so that every thought is a conscious one to realize choices—to drink or not to drink, to be happy or to be unhappy—as they are appropriate in the moment.

I wish we could give everyone a banner to put on with their clothing each morning that says, "I Practice Loyalty To Self!" to remind them to always choose to release anger and negativity and to build in happiness, attention, self-love and self-respect.

When you know you are fence sitting, it is an excellent state of mind to be in, an excellent time to practice—to practice the tools you've learned, such as written dialogue. Written dialogue puts the conflict in black and white before you. There you can recognize your conflicting beliefs and see both sides. It can make it easier to choose. The five-step prayer process brings out the truth for us and makes it easier for us to make the choices.

A fence sitter doesn't use the tools. A fence sitter is either in addictive behavior, or abstinence until he falls back into using. Fence sitters seldom fall on the right side. They usually fall back in the familiar, back in the negative, back in the destructive lifestyles.

The right side of the fence is always a conscious choice. Sometimes it is a choice that has to be remade and re-chosen daily, sometimes moment-by-moment. But it is never forced upon us and it never happens accidentally. It is never something that just happens to us. It is something that we choose because we've been given the free will to choose. We've been given that responsibility to choose. And when we choose, we're empowered, and we no longer are a victim. When we choose the side of the fence that supports our destructive lifestyles, it often feels that we don't have the power to choose differently. We choose from habit subconsciously. This only can happen when we allow ourselves to entertain conflicting beliefs.

When people no longer are willing to believe that they are addicts or alcoholics, but that they have been experiencing addictions, they find that they do have choice. Our technique removes them from themselves. We give them a chance to meet their "higher self" and to allow the "higher self" to give them permission to make a choice for self-love and self-respect. No longer do they suffer from an incurable disease. No longer are they a victim of their DNA, genetic predispositions, their painful memories or their environment. Choosing is knowing fully that we can experience being only human or we can know ourselves as spiritual beings having a human experience.

So a good choice is not whether to be a drug addict sometimes or be a child of God at other times. It is to be finished, not going back and forth, finished with sitting on that fence. It's like being in an abusive relationship with a person, getting beaten and battered, leaving and going back, believing you're needed, wanted and desired, remembering the good times, believing the promises that it will be better. It never gets better. There will come a time when you have to choose. I believe that to be free from addiction to anything or anyone each of us has to look at what we're addicted to then say clearly and intentionally and with great commitment and conviction, "I am finished with that. I am finished, and it is over and it is done." This is freedom.

An opportunity to detox

A physical obstacle to people with substance abuse problems is the lack of opportunity for a total and complete detox, an opportunity to be free from their chemical of choice in their physical body, and to not accomplish this by substituting other chemicals. It would be a period of time allowing individuals to build up their body with rest and nutrition and emotional nurturing. It would teach them that the nurturing is something that can be provided to them through individuals up to a point. It would teach them that help given through the nurturing by others must be accepted into self and used as a self-soothing technique. We can rely on the help of others up to the point that we are empowered to help ourselves.

Our experience with traditional medical detox has been that people go into a detox center for three to five days. If they are accepted they are given medicine to bring their vital signs into the normal range. Once this is accomplished, the medical people feel that a bandage has been applied, and the patient is released. As the patient goes out the door of the detox center, it is recommended that they enter a treatment program, a halfway house and attend Twelve Step meetings.

We've observed that people coming out of these medical detoxes generally are released under the influence of drugs supplied by the medical staff. Often they appear to be more "under the influence" than before they went to detox. The only difference is now they're now on medications or physician prescribed chemicals instead of street drugs or alcohol. The "bandage" is just that—a patch. A temporary solution for a permanent wound.

Many individuals go into detox centers and spend 24 hours under observation and because their vital signs are not out of the normal range, they are rejected for service and asked to leave. These individuals go to detox centers because they obviously desire to quit abusing those substances, so the rejection is an emotionally, psychologically and spiritually traumatic experience. Because they are afraid to experience withdrawal symptoms, they usually re-use or find another substance to ward off the symptoms of withdrawal. The medical detox centers primarily deal with the physical body. They may do some counseling, but in general, because these centers that are funded through insurance plans that cover only the science of medicine, not the art and science involved in the human psyche, no one leaves detox centers strong enough and safe enough to maintain the choice to stop using drugs or alcohol or destructive behavior to cover emotional pain.

What would work better is a detox facility that would keep people for a minimum of 14 days. It would be nurturing and holistic in its approach, dealing with the whole person—body, mind and spirit. It would be staffed with 24-hour supervision with a nurse or certified nursing assistant monitoring their physical condition. A naturopathic doctor, trained in addiction treatments, would be on call or on staff 24 hours a day, all day, every day, even holidays. Access to someone who really cares at this "moment of detox" is incredibly critical.

This detox center would utilize a detox acupuncture protocol, which is used in many states and at Arizona Pathways with great success. This program would use an herbal detox tea, amino acid therapy and stress and pain reducing natural supplements. *Arizona Pathways established this kind of detox center, but because we could not obtain any funding we could not keep it open and available.* This holistic model worked wonderfully and most clients were able to quickly and healthfully complete the withdrawal process. *It is my goal to open this kind of center again. This will take donors who see the need for this who will help.*

Because there are few holistic detox programs in our area of the country many of our clients seem to never really get completely clean. The few clinics using this type of detox are very expensive so not available to most people. Instead they go to medical detox, come out on medicine, and the medicine wears off in a few days. They have various periods of sobriety from zero to around 30 days, becoming a revolving door between using to detoxing with other chemicals and back to using. Our experience tells us that a real and comprehensive detox would enable many people to get off the fence and to stay off the fence. It would alleviate the fear of withdrawal symptoms. It would give them an opportunity to start feeling healthy, nurtured and encouraged and supported.

The prevailing institutional approach to addiction and recovery presents a major obstacle. Often medical and the psychiatric professionals believe that people use drugs and alcohol because they are self-medicating, that if they're prescribed legal chemicals and are taken as prescribed, they will not be driven to medicate themselves.

Our experience in having many clients who are considered "duly diagnosed," a term that means they are mentally ill substance abusers, is that they abuse the chemicals that are prescribed to them in addition to continuing to abuse the drugs of choice from the drug dealers, or continue to drink alcohol with their medication. We have seen more overdoses on prescribed medications than by illegal drug abuse. We have seen that most people who visit psychiatrists do not receive sympathetic, understanding and encouraging counseling—they receive prescriptions. They seem to be "over-medicated." Very few of these people are on one or two prescribed medications, more often it's five to seven. We see a lot of people with a lot of pills and a lot of combining those pills with alcohol, cocaine, heroin or crystal meth. We see a lot of overdoses.

One other aspect of detoxification, or leaving an old life behind, is the process of phase. In phase one, the first 30 days, our clients are restricted to living on campus. The purpose of phase one is to eliminate emotional stress and external influences. Part of giving up the influence of external influence is unplugging from all electronic communication. This includes use of cell phones, laptops, iPods, email, video games, Facebook and other social media. Only supervised phone calls from the treatment center's landline are permitted. The initial reaction from clients who are cut off from electronic communication is anger. They fear the loss of this kind of constant connection, and the fear of having to be with themselves. However, this fear when an individual gives into it and thus overcomes it is what allows them to get in touch with the "higher power" that we know is what saves them.

We see a lot of individuals afraid to switch to a "higher power" because they are convinced by medical professional that they need medications, and that they will need them forever, not something they can take for a while and then gradually stop taking. Because of the prevalence of social media and electronic communication, individuals are convinced that reliance on this kind of connection keeps them safe. These are major obstacles to getting off the fence because to believe that God is the power and the presence in their life, and to believe that they need chemicals and connection with someone beyond themselves is an enormous conflict, and when people have conflicts, they sit on the fence.

Losing losers

Another obstacle to getting off the fence is what we call the unwillingness to lose your losers. Losing your losers means to be completely honest about your thoughts, beliefs and behaviors and to honestly evaluate which ones keep you on the fence. Honesty is difficult. But its roots lie in Loyalty To Self!

To really understand what it is like to lose the losers in life, here are two stories. One is about what I witnessed with Scott. The other is about Sally's experiences at Arizona Pathways.

It was the month of August, and when it's hot, we experience a big increase in the number of people who are looking for a place to stay. After years of experience, I've gotten very intuitive about determining who is seeking help in finding freedom from destructive life choices and who is just looking for food and shelter. In the hot months, it is usual to turn away one shelter-seeker per day.

Scott walked across the parking lot that morning, just as we were finishing the morning group session. He was pulling a wheeled suitcase. As I talked with him, he was perspiring and his face was red. He said he was thirsty and hungry, and desperate. He was struggling with addiction to crystal meth, living in his broken car. He was scared and was indeed looking for help. A gut feeling encouraged me to accept him as a client and my staff members agreed.

In group, he identified himself as an addict, believing it meant he always would be an addict. Scott had a lot of other limiting beliefs. He was convinced that addiction was an incurable disease, felt that it was "too late" for him and that addiction determined his future. He was depressed because he thought he'd lost his daughter whom he hadn't seen in years. His formal education ended with the GED. His mind was filled with fear, guilt and shame, yet some spark of love of life drew him to Arizona Pathways.

Through his determined willingness to create a changed life, he applied himself to the program. Limiting and negative thoughts and beliefs were recognized as his "losers." He faced them and replaced them with positive, spiritual truths.

Today, Scott works as the program manager at Arizona Pathways. He has established a close, trusting and honest relationship with his daughter and being a father is the most natural experience for him. He works outside of Arizona Pathways to provide for his daughter and his other personal needs. He is enrolled in college and is taking courses to become a counselor for those who have problems with substance abuse. He is engaged to his girlfriend and has developed other supportive friendships. Scott has been clean and sober for more than six years.

Sally had been a "working girl" or a prostitute, and a "crack whore." She was working in our neighborhood when she learned that her ex-husband was a participant in the Arizona Pathways program because he was seeking relief from heroin addiction.

The Pathways staff asked her to stay away from the clients, but she would sneak back onto the property to see her ex, as well as other clients. One day, she asked if she could speak to me about her addiction to crack cocaine. Her appearance was typical of her lifestyle: she was skinny, drawn and gray, with lifeless eyes. Still, I could see the attractive person underneath her surface. She begged me to please give her a chance, and I did.

Sally was quite a challenge. She didn't get along well with the other female clients at first. Eventually, she let a little love in and the walls came down. She had experienced many personal losses and her limiting beliefs were: not caring about anything, believing that all that mattered to her had been lost forever, no one would want her, it was too late and she thought she was ugly. She believed she had given up everything because of her relationship with her ex-husband, the heroin addict. He had talked her into prostitution to support their drug habits. She was convinced that prostitution was better than theft, and that her ex needed her in order to stay alive. She was attached to this feeling of being needed.

It took months of tearful soul searching for Sally to feel safe enough and loved enough to discover her self-limiting and destructive beliefs that kept her in the addict's lifestyle. She became brave enough to challenge these losers and to replace them with the spiritual truth of herself as a beloved child of God. She has stayed clean and sober for over 10 years, and during this time she survived cancer, arthritis and the death of a child. She now owns a home and is going to college, studying to become a counselor.

Not long ago I took a phone call and heard her voice at the other end saying, "Hi mom!" I feel blessed to be someone she feels free to call "mom" and I'm very proud of her.

What keeps an addict attracted to the life filled with losers that they also desire to leave behind? It's not just the people they hang out with, it's their attachments to what people think about them, to how they believe they are perceived, and their attachment to their fear.

Losing the losers means being willing to let go of beliefs and fears that conflict with your perception of yourself as a spiritual child of God and your perception of yourself as safe and loved, powerful and true. Every belief that you have that tells you that you are weak, bad, or unworthy must be let go of in order to be free. Any belief that tells you that you have to go to so many meetings, take so many medications, or have so many degrees or credentials to be okay, must be let go of. Self-limiting beliefs are the losers that are able to keep you stuck in unhappiness.

Remember that you were created to individually express and experience all that God wants you to be. So the losers are not the drugs, not your friends who also use and keep you in your pattern of abuse. They are not your history or even the abuse you suffered. Your losers are how you feel about those things and how important they are to you. Losing your losers means to let go of your identification with those things. It means to let go of your attachment to what they mean to you. To let go and choose to identify and attach to your essential goodness, to accept only what provides health and helpfulness, only what allows you to experience and express yourself in a way that allows you to feel "high."

The goal is not to give up getting "high." Losing your losers does not mean that you do not get high anymore. Losing your losers means that you choose to be high most of the time without the things that destroy you and with the things God provides. God wants you to be high and you have the natural desire to be high. So losing your losers is actually releasing your attachment to beliefs and things that interfere with your being high. Of course I am referring to being really high, being high by knowing the truth and experiencing and living that truth. You and I know that the drugs lie to you and tell you that you are "high," that you are invincible, pain free and happy. But using drugs brings you lower every time you abuse them. *It is natural to want to be lied to when you are suffering pain that you experience as unbearable.* This is the real purpose of these chemicals that are prescribed.

While some of you are reading or listening to this, you may have this little voice that says, "When I understand all of this and I see myself as a child of God and not as an addict/alcoholic anymore, I can drink again, right?" The answer to that question is, theoretically, yes. But we don't live in theory. We live in experience. And if your goal is to participate in this philosophy so you can drink again, you are going to find yourself falling off the fence on the wrong side. If your goal is to be free from the desire to drink alcohol, free from the desire to medicate, free to do what God created you to do, then the question would not even be asked, if you can drink again or not. It would be irrelevant. It would not be important to you.

If you ask the questions, "Can I drink again? Can I use drugs again? Can I engage in addictive behavior again?" it reveals what is important to you. So practically, no, you can't drink again because it would not be a wise decision. When you build up a strong reserve of Loyalty To Self, you will not even need to ask those questions.

Addiction vocabulary

For people struggling with addictions, vocabulary itself is very dishonest. I hear words like "getting a fix." In truth, you are really getting more broken each time you get a fix. It is a lie. Likewise people with alcohol, heroin and pain medication addictions get sick once their bodies become physically dependent on that substance of choice, and I hear them say "I just need to get well." Again another lie. You are not getting well, you are getting sicker.

Every time you refuse to go through the withdrawal experience because you don't want to be physically ill, you say you are getting well. But what you are doing is tightening the chain of bondage to the substance.

Clients describe how their body gets so excited when they even think about using their substance of choice, or if they hear a "trigger" word, or go to a familiar place related to their use of substances. They talk about how their stomach starts churning and how they feel that sense of excitement. But what is your body telling you? When your body senses that you are thinking about using, when it senses that something is triggered, that concept of getting more of your substance of choice, is that eager anticipation, or revulsion? When your stomach starts churning and you get diarrhea and you start sweating and your palms are wet, is that the joy of true anticipation? Or is your body saying, "Please, no more!" Pay close attention to the real message. Abusers ignore. Healthy individuals pay attention and do not ignore the "Please, no more!" message.

Another example of deceptive language is: "Let's party." I've seen a lot of people in bondage to chemicals and they are not having fun; they are not "partying." Even under the influence, they are not happy or joyful. They may be numb, they may be totally unaware of what is going on, but they are not experiencing a party of real joy and happiness. I know that many individuals begin drinking and drugging in pursuit of the fun of escaping reality, and it might feel fun until they find that they are addicted. No matter how hard they chase after that initial "fun" it eludes them, and they continue to chase that first "high" while actually destroying themselves.

Fear and faith

The Bible teaches if you have as much faith as a grain of mustard seed, you can move mountains. Likewise if you have as much fear as a grain of mustard seed, there is power in drugs and alcohol to addict you, that if you drink alcohol or abuse a drug again or if you participate in a behavior that has caused destruction, if you have any fear at all, even as little as a mustard seed, that is enough fear or enough faith to put you back into bondage.

Fear is the belief that what you don't want to happen will happen, and faith is believing that what you desire to happen will happen. If you continue to believe that addictions to chemicals or destructive behaviors have the power to destroy your life, you are right! So Arizona Pathways' program is about freedom from the desire to use, not how to learn to use addictive substances without problems.

Chapter 9:

Problems of Addiction Recovery Treatment Programs and Plans

It is impossible to talk about the next step in treating addiction and the promise it holds without discussing the failures of the current techniques commonly in use today. There are three main problems in the current approach:

1. How punishment is used as treatment.
2. Using legal drugs to solve the problem of addiction.
3. Bureaucratic systems meant to help treat addiction often end up interfering with real treatment.

The common medical model, as has been discussed, labels addiction as a disease—and not just a disease, but an incurable disease. The afflicted are taught that they were born with or contracted it and must learn to manage the symptoms. Like having diabetes, if you take the medicine, eat the prescribed diet and so on, you can live a normal life. But unlike diabetes, if an addicted person displays the symptoms of their disease—the craving and pursuit of substances or their behavior while under the influence of it—that is a crime for which they will likely be punished.

Punishment as treatment

The business of both legal and illegal drugs is tied to the system of addiction and punishment as well. Huge sums are spent on law enforcement to try to slow the transport and supply of illegal drugs. A small fraction of both public and private money is spent to slow the demand. Relatively no funding is allotted for treatment for those who wish to face and control their addictive behavior, either in or out of prison. The alcohol and drug business is big business. The prison business is big business. The two businesses are deeply related; both are growing and rely on addicted people to continue to grow. An overwhelming percentage of crimes are committed by people under influence of drugs or alcohol.

There are voices that speak on behalf of a treatment solution, who understand the enemy is not drugs but demand for drugs, but it has yet to become policy on a national level. Businesses that profit from prisons have little incentive to support use of their funding for treatment instead.

In order to evaluate the current approach to drug abuse and addiction, it's important to be aware of how dysfunctional the judicial and penal system is for dealing with it. The criminal justice system will send thousands of addicted citizens to prison for two to 10 years for drug or drug related charges at $35,000 per year or more. There is no plan, infrastructure or public policy to pay for treatment that could be half the cost, or even less, of imprisonment. Even if addicts manage to get some kind of treatment, the best they can hope for is 30 days of treatment.

Here's a contrary idea: If the system sentenced people instead to 30 days of incarceration as punishment for drug related crimes, and 1-5 years of treatment for their addiction, imagine the money and lives that could be saved.

I know about prison systems from my clients and from my

own visits to Arizona prisons, and assume they are similar in other states. I wonder how many people know how common drug use is in prison. I wonder how many people know that prison gangs largely run prisons. Do they know that inmates teach others how to commit crimes? There is very little real education offered by the prison system, but there are a lot of teachers among the inmate population and then that 'education' propels future criminal behavior.

Prisons provide a perfect environment to learn how to become a drug addict. People don't know how to use these drugs until someone teaches them, or "turns them on." Both in and out of prison, one addict turns a newcomer into a user/addict for selfish reasons, usually to create access to the resources of the newcomer. This is one way prison dealers expand their market. It also expands the opportunities for the already addicted to ensure the needed continuous supply for him or herself. This practice isn't stopped by being in prison; it's more pervasive.

Prisons also efficiently provide education from inmate to inmate in all of the latest scams, fraudulent schemes and other illegal activities. Often, strong friendships are developed based on negative experiences and beliefs that continue after release from prison.

Drugs find their way inside prisons. How can these individuals be expected to leave the negative environment of prison, with little or no preparation to transition back into society, with little or no time clean from substance abuse to be successful outside the prison walls? It is not surprising that many return to prison again and again. Each time they return the sentence is longer. Some of these people are now doing 10 or more years, yet have never received treatment for their addiction.

Once they are released, they usually have very few options. The lucky ones have skills or trades that they developed prior to incarceration. Some are able to work while in prison because of these skills. Prisoners must be cleared to work and are paid a very small wage. These kinds of jobs are the equivalent of sweatshop work, but the prisoners are happy to have something to do. Many of them save this money toward a new chance at life beyond prison. Because of their experience, some can find jobs when they are released. But others find that many employers will not hire felons. Many landlords will not rent to felons. Many end up in shelters or on the streets, and the return to prison is always close. A person who is convicted of a drug crime is not eligible for food stamps, even after they've served their sentence.

Prisons don't provide addicted persons what they need to break away from their revolving doors, and maybe that can't be their job. Or maybe it can. Upon re-entering society after prison, many people are helpless. Some have families who take them in and support them. Some have connections for employment. But those who come out and find few or no options have no voice. This is a message that society needs to recognize. If addicts are to live with love and light, without the need to experience pain to experience pleasure, then they must learn to forgive themselves of having a mistaken identity. And when they can leave this identity behind, and experience true healing, then society will also forgive them. After forgiveness comes compassion.

What is needed are transitional programs to provide a real chance at freedom—including treatment for their addiction, life skills training, mental and physical health care, education assistance and opportunities. They also need a safe community to adjust to living in society. These programs would cost much less than continuous incarceration. These are not just bad people that society needs protection from—they are our mothers, fathers, brothers, sisters, sons and daughters. They deserve our support and encouragement. Punishment for suffering from the "disease" of addiction by incarceration doesn't work, is destructive and very expensive.

Where can we start to get a public policy on this? If you are reading this book, please give some thought as to how you can be the change you want to see in terms of help for addiction and all the consequences of addiction. Perhaps we can find a way through politics. Perhaps we can find a way through the private system, such as through funding from foundations. Perhaps we can find a way just through spreading the word, person-to-person that the problems of addiction will not go away until we believe that the entire issue can be solved.

Addictive behavior in adults is often the result when a person felt unloved as a child. A ten-year study by Vincent Felitti, M.D. and Robert Anda, M.D. produced the science to prove this. When a child is not loved or cared for, or when they have suffered the trauma of Adverse Childhood Experiences (see www.acestudy. org), they look to addiction to fill what is missing in their psyche. Of course, too much "love" lavished on a child can be damaging as well. Children who are overly protected, worried over and given everything their heart desires may grow up to use addiction to fill the space of need created by having too much of this kind of conditional (as opposed to unconditional) love.

This must be recognized by more people and especially by addicts themselves. Healing is possible.

An article in the *Arizona Republic* newspaper (February 29, 2008) had the headline "U.S. Leads World with its Prison Population." It stated that for the first time in history, more than one in every hundred American adults was in jail. According to a report released by the Penn Center and cited in the article, 50 states spent more than $49 billion on jails and prisons last year incarcerating low risk offenders, despite no improvement in recidivism or overall crime. In some states, crime increased by only 3 percent in the past thirty years, while the inmate population has increased by 600 percent.

It is likely that addiction to drugs and alcohol has increased to account for these alarming statistics.

Another recent newspaper article I read told of a man who was arrested for driving under the influence of alcohol (DUI). The judge ordered him to complete a treatment program or go to jail. Which option is paid for by the criminal justice system? Jail, of course. So if treatment is the option the offender prefers, he must find a way to pay for it. This is one of the reasons there is a majority of minority people in prison. They have fewer options because they have less money.

I've been asked why people don't just go to treatment when they realize they have become chemically addicted and/or dependent instead of continuing with the destructive lifestyle until they end up in prison. One of the main answers is that affordable and effective treatment is not available to those without money to pay. Incarceration is free in that there are no immediate out-of-pocket expenses for the addict. Unfortunately, incarceration is not free to society and consumes a major portion of Arizona's budget. This is true for other states' budgets as well.

Here is a story to illustrate how disconnected the system is. One of my clients, who was on probation and had a history of alcoholism, got drunk. His probation officer found that he'd violated his probation and he was sent to prison, this time for three years. He was hard working, helpful and was making progress, but had relapsed. What had reappeared in his life to cause the relapse and the jail consequence were either the symptoms of his "incurable disease" or the deeply held destructive belief about himself that he was unworthy of love or that his pain could not be healed. In any event, the probation system required punishment. While in prison he would occasionally write to us at the center.

One day I got a phone call from him. He was scared and begged me to send $50 to a dealer here in Phoenix. He'd gotten involved with heroin in prison, owed $50 for drugs and was in physical danger unless he paid. I considered the information he gave me, then called the police. An officer who worked on gangs and drugs in the neighborhood said, "Send the money."

I asked him if he wanted the name and address of the dealer. His response was "Oh, I guess." He never followed up on it. Having experienced similar situations later, I came to know this approach on the part of law enforcement was not uncommon. I asked him why he never followed up. He said that this happens all the time and the police department does not have the resources to combat this issue.

Another time, a client told me he had given his car to his drug dealer and that he had to pay him $200 by noon the next day or the car was going to Mexico. The car was valuable, and he said if I would get it from the drug dealer he would donate it to our program. His mother in California said she would send us the signed and notarized title overnight express, thanked me for helping her son and said she was pleased our program would benefit. So I went with the client and paid $200 to retrieve the car.

Then I called the police to alert them about this drug dealer, who the client had been buying heroin from at this same location for over 10 years. I thought the police would want to know. They were not interested. This again illustrates the lack of power and resources in the current law enforcement system.

The business of drugs and its effects locally and internationally are in the news now every day. Almost all of the abused drugs in Arizona come through Mexico, including marijuana, heroin, cocaine, methamphetamine and prescription medications. Our government gives billions of dollars to Mexico to help them fight drug cartels. With what is known about the corruption in the Mexican government and police force, one wonders how this money is used and who benefits from it and if it is possible to ever win a "war on drugs."

Government policies are designed to reduce the supply of drugs and they spend fortunes in the attempt. Laws of supply and demand thwart this attempt because even when supply is reduced and demand stays the same, prices go up, more crime is committed, with more theft, violence, criminal behavior, prisons and drug use.

The "war on drugs" policy is misnamed. We can't win a war if we can't identify the enemy. Drugs are not the enemy. Drugs are chemicals that of themselves are not able to destroy us or even threaten to destroy us. Some drugs, when used in the right way for the right reasons, prevent suffering and support healing. The real enemy is the individual's belief in the power of drugs, the desire for drugs, the addiction to drugs.

If drugs could be purchased legally, much of the excitement of "getting away with something" or being the "connection" for others would be gone. This excitement can be a major attraction to young people and first time drug abusers. Drugs could also be controlled for quality and consistency; people wouldn't be risking injecting chemicals that they don't know are used to "cut" and process the street drugs.

After more than 20 years of treating people who abuse drugs and alcohol, I have an opinion about the way our society has historically treated the abuse that results when people try to fill a need, a hurt, a want in their psyche. Society attempts to control. Society prohibits. Society punishes.

I advocate the legalization of drugs such as marijuana, heroin and cocaine but not methamphetamines. There already are pharmaceutical quantities of these drugs that people purchase both legally and illegally, and still abuse. These pharmaceutical drugs don't sound as bad as the plant-based drugs. For either type of drug, plant-based or pharmaceutical, there is very little education about the lethal dose and the probable dependency that ensues after prolonged use and abuse.

There is no education for how to get off any of these drugs.

There is no funding for treatment and detox.

The honest truth must be told about these drugs and if people choose to use them, they should be provided with education about using them and told that if they become addicted, they will absolutely need help to get off of them.

If drugs were legal, they could be taxed. Quality and quantity could be regulated which would eliminate the violence of the cartels and the street gangs. The impact on law enforcement and prisons would lessen, saving money in order to provide education and treatment.

Prohibition does not work.

What does work are the tools of the heart. Love, compassion and forgiveness. And treatment programs work when they are based on these principals.

One of the main objections to the legalization of drugs is the fear that even more people will become addicted. We are already experiencing an epidemic of substance abuse and addiction involving legal drugs and alcohol. It's not clear there would be more drug use arising from legalization, but reducing the violence and criminal activity and the cost of incarceration and judicial expenses relating to substance abuse and addictions outweigh the risk of a potential increase in people choosing to use addictive substances. Prohibition of alcohol did not keep people from drinking. The prohibition provided a market for the gangsters and created related violence and resulted in deaths. Repealing the prohibition laws didn't cause more alcoholism. Increased revenue from legal production, distribution and sales contributes much revenue for our government.

The money and lives saved by removing the criminal aspects, plus the revenue that could be generated through taxation and regulation of these drugs, would provide ample resources for real education and treatment. If drugs were legal to process, market, sell and use by licensed and regulated businesses, the primary substances could be purchased directly from growers and harvesters, providing legitimate income without the violence and the cost expended attempting to eradicate the supply. This would eliminate drug cartels that in turn often support terrorists and terrorism at a huge cost in resources and lives. This would stop bloodshed and destruction related to the drug business and drug wars. Prisons would have fewer inmates, at less taxpayer cost. The economy would benefit by the creation of new jobs to procure, process and market these drugs. Profits related to the sale of these drugs and tax and license revenue would provide funds for prevention and addiction treatment, which would also create jobs.

No one really wants to be addicted to alcohol or drugs, but once a person is inside addiction, getting out is not easy. Until the consciousness of society changes so that people no longer look outside of themselves for freedom from physical, mental and emotional pain—people will continue abusing chemicals. As long as we address addiction with deprivation and punishment, instead of a natural fulfillment and support, substance abuse will continue.

Legal drugs are not safe drugs

We are a society that relies heavily on prescription drugs for legitimate purposes as well as questionable purposes, such as treating drug abuse. The truth about the dangers of prescribed medication is finally getting some attention. We know that elementary school kids often sell their Ritalin or trade for Oxycontin. Many adults at Arizona Pathways with addictions to crystal meth or methamphetamine were prescribed and took Ritalin as children. News headlines detail the death of entertainers from overdoses and combinations of legally prescribed medications. In our program we've seen commonly prescribed painkillers Vicodin and Oxycontin highly abused, and their abuse often leads to heroin addiction.

With managed health care, medical doctors have only about 10 to 15 minutes with a patient, just long enough to listen to the patient's report of what hurts, how bad it hurts on a scale of 1-10, and what drug to prescribe to alleviate the symptoms.

For people with addictions, level of pain often is cited as an 11. It's easy to understand why drug addicts love their doctors. Not only can they get lots of drugs, enough to use and often enough to sell, usually paid for by the taxpayer or insurance companies, they also get the satisfaction of outsmarting the doctor. This ability to manipulate a highly educated, intelligent person can also be a "high," a boost of self-esteem boost to the lowly addict.

One of the current medical practices in hospital detoxification units is to provide the detox patient with a psychiatric evaluation and then to prescribe several psychotropic medications that match the labels revealed in their diagnosis. When a person is withdrawing from chemical dependency they usually will display symptoms that look like evidence of mental and emotional disorders. Labeling someone "bipolar," "manic-depressive," "schizophrenic," "borderline" or other handing them some of the other psychological disorders, and prescribing drugs to treat these labels seems crazy.

No one should be evaluated for mental illness until they are "clean and sober" for at least six months, preferably a year. Most displays of what look like mental health disorders disappear with sobriety, nurturing, exercise and counseling. There probably is no one on a detox unit that doesn't suffer anxiety while they are experiencing withdrawal. It's a huge mistake to label them with an anxiety disorder under those circumstances.

The best way to illustrate the problems of treating addiction with more drugs is with some examples, which I offer from my direct experience.

A social worker from one of our local hospitals called to ask about our program. A patient in the chemical dependency unit was interested in entering our program when she was released from the hospital. I was asked to come to the hospital to interview her. She liked our philosophy and agreed to be released to us in two days.

I then asked about her medications and was given a list of seven different psychotropic drugs. I asked the client if she had been taking these drugs before she was admitted to the hospital. She said only one, a common antidepressant. I asked her what reason was given to take the other six. She said she didn't know, so I asked to speak with her nurse or someone who could explain to us why the additional medications were prescribed.

Suddenly, I was asked to leave and was told that the hospital would not refer patients to our program because I was advising them not to take the prescribed medications. I had not advised the patient not to take the drugs, but I had wanted to know what she was prescribed, and why, and that the patient be informed about the reasons that she was being medicated.

This patient did enter our program and because of the reaction of the hospital staff she called the doctor herself to ask about the medications. Ultimately, she decided to take only the one medication she had taken prior to her hospitalization. She worked on her nutrition with the naturopathic doctors at our clinic, stayed clean and sober, and left the program after one year to marry and move to Colorado where she is doing well. She is one of thousands I've seen who have come through Arizona Pathways who are overly prescribed.

Common treatment of behavioral health problems, including substance abuse, is to chemically restrain the individual's behavior, then release them to find a place to go. That place often is the streets, which often leads to jail, a homeless shelter, re-hospitalization or death. The hospital stay usually is from a few days to two weeks. The hospital, pharmacy, drug manufacturers and staff all get paid for treating these patients for a short time. Then the patients are released under the influence of legal drugs to fend for themselves. So they enter a revolving door that never provides independence and freedom.

One of the most lethal classifications of prescribed drugs is benzodiazepine. Librium and Valium were the first benzodiazepines introduced. These drugs are tranquilizers, and when used properly, they are useful to people experiencing short-term anxiety and trauma. Benzodiazepines are addictive and millions of people have become dependent on them. There have long been concerns about over-prescribing and extended, repeat prescriptions by doctors long past the period when they are actually benefiting the patient.

Today, there are approximately 20 benzodiazepines currently available. Ativan, Klonopin and Xanax are the three with which I am most familiar, and because they are readily available and preferred by the alcoholic and drug-addicted population. When ingested in combination with alcohol, methadone, heroin, cocaine or meth, they have the effect of enhancing the "high" of the drug of choice. Unfortunately, they often cause death when used with other chemicals. Benzodiazepines also produce the experience of "blackouts" (no conscious awareness) when taken more than prescribed. Irrational behavior follows which often leads to arrest or other problems. Overdose of these drugs often leads to respiratory failure and death.

The first client I knew who died of a drug overdose was Joe. He was in his mid thirties, a chronic alcoholic who also smoked pot and used heroin on occasion. Joe worked as a framer in construction. He was a talented musician, singing and songwriting, playing piano and guitar.

When I first met Joe he was a hardcore alcoholic. His tolerance for alcohol was unbelievable. He looked like a longhaired hippie. He had been abusing chemicals since he was a child. Kind, creative, intelligent, funny, compassionate, moody, hard working are all words that describe Joe. He was a father who loved his son. I was not aware that he was seeing a counselor who was prescribing Ativan.

One night after work, Joe came home, had dinner, and seemed perfectly fine. I thought he had gone to bed early as he usually did, because he worked early in the morning. So it was a total shock when the white car pulled into my driveway the next morning. Two men in business suits came to my door. They then told me that Joe had been found dead in a motel room of an overdose of alcohol, heroin and benzodiazepines. I doubt Joe would have even gone out that night if he hadn't been taking Ativan and alcohol, both legal drugs.

Ted, a 53 year-old, long-term heroin addict, also died because he was taking methadone and using Xanax to enhance the methadone. He died of an overdose of methadone and Xanax, both legal prescription drugs. Chronic heroin addicts have told me that methadone is not really a treatment for heroin. Heroin addicts can get methadone maintenance treatment for free, so often use it as an "insurance policy" to avoid getting sick if they go into withdrawal because they can't get heroin.

Though the common belief is that addicts can't get high on methadone, in reality they can. The legal limit on dosage is so high that it takes years to get to the level that no longer produces euphoria. But addicted people are very resourceful. They have discovered that "benzos" combined with methadone create euphoria. They also know that if they add heroin or cocaine to the methadone, they can create the high that they want, something that is also a recipe for death. When waiting for a client at a methadone clinic on two different occasions, I was asked if I had "benzos" to sell or if I wanted to buy some.

It's taken years to learn from these "master teachers" just how dangerous legal drugs are. Learning that some of them were abusing medications, I often went to doctor's appointments with them and made sure that they were honest about their drug abuse and particularly if they had a history of abusing prescribed medications.

Eddie was one of the best teachers. He loved pills, especially if he could take them with heroin or methadone. Before I knew about these pills, I noticed one day that Eddie was acting in a very bizarre manner. He was in constant motion, agitated and hostile and sweating profusely. He wouldn't tell me what he had taken, but another client told me that he had gotten some "pills." I took him to two emergency rooms, asking for help, and spent several hours, only to be told that they couldn't do anything. I was referred to the mental health crisis unit, so we spent four hours there, waiting to talk with someone.

Eddie was in constant motion, constantly complaining, acting "crazy." When we were called to the window, the staff person was clearly afraid of Eddie, told me to be careful, and said they couldn't help. They had no way to treat people who abuse the medicine that they prescribe. I stayed with him until the drugs wore off because if I left him on the street, he would probably have hurt someone or have gotten hurt himself. After that, I learned what benzo intoxication looked like. So I made sure that every doctor who treated Eddie or any of our clients knew not to prescribe benzos. We do not allow them at Arizona Pathways when they are prescribed, even though they are legal.

Like many others, Eddie went to be evaluated by our state mental health program. They diagnosed him as having an anxiety disorder. The prescribed medication was Klonopin, a benzodiazepine. I took Eddie to the doctor, and, together, we explained his drug use history and his previous abuse of the benzos. The doctor wrote a note in big red letters on Eddie's file—"do not prescribe benzodiazepines because of history of abuse." Several months later, Eddie had an appointment at that same doctor's office. I sent him with a form authorizing the release of information relating to any prescribed medication for him. When he returned, he said he didn't see the doctor, and had only talked with the nurse and caseworker. He returned the form saying that he wasn't given any medication.

The next day, Eddie said that he was going to lunch with a friend, someone I knew and trusted to be alone with Eddie but Eddie didn't come home that night. He had been here ten years, had moved out twice but returned because he needed the support of this program. Never, in all that time, had Eddie not returned home at night.

I called his case manager at the mental health clinic. She told me that Eddie had been there the day before and that a new doctor had seen him. I asked her if he had been prescribed any medication, and she said yes, he had been provided with 90 Klonopin. I asked her how that had happened, knowing the file had the notation regarding Eddie's history of abusing this particular medication. She offered no explanation and asked me to call her when Eddie returned.

Monday afternoon a white car drove up and two men dressed in business suits—plainclothes police officers—came to my door. Both Eddie and his companion had been found dead in an alley. They were identified by their fingerprints because their identification and anything of value were gone, even their shoes. I needed to help them find the next of kin. One doctor, one bottle of pills, two dead men. I don't think they would have been out there using the drugs at all if they hadn't been given the 90 pills. The pills were free, paid for by taxpayers and legal through the state's mental health clinic.

I can tell you the experiences of over a dozen people I knew personally who died because of these pills. One of the effects of benzos is that they seem to awaken the craving for other drugs of choice. Eddie had been clean and sober for almost a year when he died. He had almost embraced his freedom from addiction. Of all the clients I have worked with, almost everyone who had been prescribed benzos had at least once (several more than once) overdosed on their medication. It is so common that I can't believe that there haven't been changes made in how these medications are prescribed.

After becoming aware of the prevalence of overdoses with benzos, I went to the hospital near our facility. I explained my concern about this situation, and asked them if they would provide me with information relating to the percentage of patients that they treat for drug overdoses related to ingested benzos. I didn't ask for names, gender or age, just what percentage. I was told to give them a few days. A few days later, the hospital called and told me that their legal department had told them not to provide that information to me. They gave me no reason, but they must not have wanted me to know that my suspicions were valid.

I was becoming aware, and I wanted to make the world aware of how deadly legal drugs can be. I wanted to make others know of this widespread and very unfortunate circumstance. Parents especially fall into this trap. They believe that their child will be safe if they can find a prescribed medication to treat their anxiety or pain.

Young people, just beginning to abuse, really concern me. Pills are often their drugs of choice because they appear clean and legal; they have a false sense of safety. I've talked to many of them, and they have no fear because they think these are safe, pharmaceutical quality drugs. They are shocked when I tell them about the people who have died using this "safe" medication.

Pain pills such as Vicodin, Percoset, Darvoset, morphine, Oxycontin and Zohydro (new in 2012 and ten times more potent than Vicodin) are in high demand for abuse. They are easy to obtain, overly prescribed, often found in medicine cabinets and sold in schools, offices, bars and on the streets. They are highly available and addictive and often cause respiratory failure due to overdose. They are also often used in combination with benzodiazapines, alcohol and methadone.

I have been told by clients who became addicted to methamphetamine (and a type of methamphetamine, methylphenidate, is labeled as Ritalin for ADHD) that they realized that they had become dependent on opiates because the illegal drug dealers cut meth with heroin so that unsuspecting users will become doubly addicted. You will not get sick from meth withdrawal but you will get sick from heroin withdrawal even if you don't know you are using it. Opiate dependency causes people to become very sick if they are not getting their "fix," so this guarantees repeat business for the dealer and manufacturer.

I received a call from a 38-year-old man asking for help to detox from methadone, benzodiazpines and pain pills. He told me he had been addicted to heroin but hadn't used heroin for five years. He also told me he had chronic back pain and was living on social security disability. Although the drugs he was currently dependent on are legal, he was trying to find a way to not continue his dependency. The medical detox facilities would not accept him because of the methadone. He was currently taking 130 mg. daily and the medical detox facilities would not accept him until he had reduced that to 30 mg. The methadone clinic did not want to reduce the dose because it keeps them in business. It is worth noting that methadone clinics make large profits and may not have an interest in reducing the need for their product. The doctor did not want to bring down his dose and they told him he could only lessen his dose by three to five milligrams per week. It's almost impossible to get the dose reduced by the 100 milligrams necessary for this person to enter medical detoxification.

Every time he expresses any discomfort to the methadone clinic, they encourage him to increase, not decrease, the dosage. He like many others is caught in a trap of legal drugs. Being on disability, he has no way to pay for any alternative solution. These legal drugs become a trap that is being presented as a solution to people who have become addicted to heroin or other opiates.

A young lady who was a client had a long history of chemical abuse and eating disorders. She was also dually diagnosed as mentally ill. This young lady became very unmanageable. She was taking seven prescribed medications. They were prescribed for pain, anticonvulsants, antidepressants, antibiotics, sedatives, sleep and muscle relaxers. Many of the side effects she had were what all these pills were supposed to be treating. Some of these medications were very addictive. She would obtain these prescriptions by complaining, "I'm in pain, I'm depressed, I can't sleep, I don't feel good, I have nightmares."

Her behavior was out of control. She was either sleeping or raging in anger. She became chemically dependent on the narcotic pain pills that were prescribed continuously for more than a year. The side effects of this medication include addiction, agitation, confusion, hostility, water retention, mood and behavior changes, nervousness, hallucinations, back pain, excessive depression, paranoia, muscle pain, cramps, abnormal dreaming and thinking, delusions, emotional instability and euphoria, headaches, nausea, upset stomach, sleeplessness, anxiety and on and on. With all these side effects, I believe this client was being very truthful in her complaints. I also observe that she experienced almost all of the mentioned side effects of her medications.

What is especially frustrating is knowing that, without private insurance, it is tax money that pays for the doctors, medications and institutions that keep this client in her painful situation. The negative results of these medications have kept her so out of control that she needed to be in a supervised and controlled environment, so she often had periods when she would be admitted to a psychiatric hospital. The hospital kept her continually even more medicated, at a daily rate of $1,000 to $3,000 per day. She would be kept until the system determined that she had been there long enough and they wouldn't pay any more, a decision that was made based on how many days she was hospitalized, not on how well she was doing. This happened due to the dictates of her insurance plan. Then she was released to a private program such as Arizona Pathways. It's not necessary to be medically trained to know how terribly wrong this is. My suggestion to all of these professionals who were being paid to care for her was to detox her from all medications. They seemed to be hurting her more than helping her.

It is easy to see that these patients become convinced that they need the medication. They have been addicted for many years, and they'd like to believe that the pills will help them. This client, her mother and I, asked the doctor at the hospital to begin to detox her from the medications and evaluate her for appropriate treatment. The psychiatrist at that hospital simply said, "We have conflicting theories." In other words, he believed she needed the medications. Even though the client was 30 years old, he refused to help her detox from the medications. Without help, she continued to use street drugs, alcohol and prescribed medication until, at taxpayer expense, she ended up in the Arizona State Prison.

There was another young man, an alcoholic, who left our program and got hit by a truck. He had serious injuries that cost the taxpayers hundreds of thousands of dollars in medical expenses. Even five years later, he continues to get free narcotic pain medication. He also has been in and out of psychiatric hospitals at taxpayer expense. He continues to get more and more prescribed, addictive medications. There are no resources for treatment, but huge amounts to support the theory that the pills will make him better, despite the obvious failure of that approach.

It's time to become aware and intolerant of this system of prescribing drugs for people with a history of substance abuse, of their loss of independence and health and of the deadly and costly overdoses on these legal drugs. It is a cycle that many of our brothers and sisters are caught in, and the system uses tax dollars to help the pharmaceutical companies and the medical companies make a profit without regard for what is really happening to these precious souls.

The problem with bureaucracy

Having treated so many clients for addiction, I have endured a lot of frustration with bureaucracy, and for a long time.

Before 2008, in a newspaper article about the health care scandal at Walter Reed Army Medical Center, Arizona

Congressman Harry Mitchell joined forces with Senators Barack Obama and Claire McCaskill to introduce the "Dignity for Wounded Warriors Act" which outlined measures to help soldiers navigate the bureaucracy. What does this tell us? Does anyone really believe creating more bureaucracy will help? Sometimes when something is broken it just can't be fixed. It must be replaced. No one likes to deal with the "system." It matters not if it is local, state, federal or corporate.

Even some religions are bogged down in rules, regulations, policy and procedures. Somewhere, sometime, leaders evolved through experience, training and personal skills and created a way to govern the general public. I think it used to work when it was simpler. Now we have been convinced that experts are only created by academia. Postgraduate degrees are now required in almost all professions. It seems like most of our government leaders feel they need to protect the citizens from every possible negative situation. Of course we all know they can't think of every possible situation so they will never succeed in totally protecting society. But they are trained to protect against liability—so whatever does happen is not their fault or responsibility. This CYA (cover your ass) mentality blocks or complicates our efforts to serve the public, run a business and live without fear of lawsuits. This fear-based mentality creates most of the red tape we get so frustrated with. It greatly interferes with the desired results of providing services. CYA makes it almost impossible to UCS (Use Common Sense). It is no wonder our government is so ineffective, our schools can't teach what and how the students can benefit most from. Health care and mental health care are too costly and not available to all who need it.

Do you know how many professions require a Ph.D. or at least a Masters level degree? Who decided that academia is the only way people can learn and become competent in many professions?

Not too long ago, you could apply for licenses, certifications and employment based on education, experience or a combination of the two. That has changed recently and everyone who wants to have a successful career in most fields is now required to have college degrees.

In my own personal experience, I worked in accounting positions for years before I went to college to study accounting. I learned on the job and I learned well. When I went to college I was able to test out of several of the required classes. Then I changed interests and decided to study Spirituality, so I ended up as an ordained minister. Then I began working with the addicted and was able to apply to take the national test to become a certified substance abuse counselor. Based on my experience and high school diploma, I passed the exam and was certified. A couple of years ago the state changed from certified to licensed. I was grandfathered in at the highest level of licensure for a substance abuse counselor, a Licensed Independent Substance Abuse Counselor (L.I.S.A.C.). Now for that license a master level degree is required, regardless of your experience.

I feel this is a big mistake. If a person can learn through experience, education, self-education, etc. what is required to pass the licensing exam in any profession, they should be accepted with the same dignity and respect as the person who has earned the master level degree. There are many ways to learn. College is very expensive and takes lots of time and effort. Some people learn better by hands-on training. Currently our young people are being convinced that college is required for success in almost any field. Students are graduating with thousands of dollars of debt for student loans, a degree, no experience and little qualification for employment. More people are going to college because of this thinking and the costs related to academia are going up. I think that the academia "nuts" are creating their own bubble in the economy.

The Arizona Pathways solution

After many years operating Arizona Pathways residential program, I realized that the funding sources for services for these people would only support licensed programs. We purchased a building in 2000 for the purpose of providing naturopathic detoxification services for our clients. We felt this would be very helpful because there are very few detox programs available and the ones that do exist use a medical model that hasn't proven to be the best for some people. We found that naturopathic detox worked better for most.

When we began this program I contacted the state to determine if we were required to be licensed. I was told that there is not a license for a naturopathic detox program. We found that the service was well received and successful and we always had clients requesting admission to the program. Unfortunately, there is no funding source available and most of our clients are not able to pay for the service. So eventually we could not keep the services available. Already owning the building, we decided to license a 30-90 day residential treatment program at that location, thinking we could then contract with the state mental health provider to provide substance abuse treatment to individuals who desire treatment but have no means to pay for it.

It took us over two years to complete all the requirements regarding the building, policies and procedures, staffing, training, inspections, and so on. Finally we were awarded the license. Thousands of dollars, blood, sweat and tears and frustration, but we did it.

The requirements are extensive. We could treat five adults who had gotten caught in the trap of chemical addiction, but who were not considered mentally challenged. We were required to provide a locked drawer or box for each client, though we would have preferred not to as these people have a history of possessing drugs. We were three square feet short of space in one bedroom so we had to move a wall. We lowered windows so someone could get out in case of fire, with hard-wired smoke detectors, and emergency lighting. We agreed to pay a registered dietitian to review a sample menu, and to post client rights in Spanish, even though we would not be accepting non-English speaking clients. We agreed to include clients in menu planning and that to post menus and keep them on file for the state to inspect. My assessment is that it would take at least one full time staff member to assure we were compliant with all these rules and regulations.

An exception to laws regarding client confidentiality, the state was to have complete access to our files. Regulations required incident reports to be filed regarding clients leaving without permission, and almost every little thing such as a disagreement, or when someone didn't eat their dinner, that happens. I realized that accepting a license meant giving up a lot of freedom to operate the program according to our personal philosophy. Still, I was willing to comply with the hope that we would be awarded a provider contract to help people who had no resources to pay for their treatment.

So, after we received our license, we registered with the State Department of Health Services, obtained a National Provider Identification number, increased our insurance coverage to cover everybody's asses and applied for a provider contract. The mental health agency sent a representative to visit our facility. She seemed pleased and positive, yet about 30 days later we received a letter saying that they already had adequate services contracted, they didn't need our five beds at this time, and our information would be kept on file in case the need for additional substance abuse treatment should arise.

I called the person who sent the letter and asked him what I should do to help all of the individuals who contact our program every week desiring treatment but have no means to pay. I told him that even their own case managers call me every week asking me to accept clients. He told me to tell whoever contacts us that we were not a contracted provider and to call their toll-free number. I asked him what would happen in response to that call. He told me that they would be put on a list, then the local office would be contacted, and then the local office would contact the client to set an appointment for an evaluation.

Whoever set up this policy has no idea what someone finally seeking help really needs, no idea what "a moment of clarity" is for the chemically dependent, addicted person. When someone who is actively abusing chemicals asks for help, it is an emergency situation. It can be life or death and help must be available immediately. There is no way someone in this situation is capable of calling an 800 number, getting on a list and waiting for an appointment for an evaluation. These people usually don't have telephones or addresses. They will continue to abuse themselves until they overdose or go to jail.

If they are or become incarcerated, the costs will not come out of the budget of the behavioral health department, but out of the justice system or the medical system. This broken system is not about providing services but about budgets and numbers.

In mid-2000s, the license that Arizona Pathways was granted expired. For some reason it was granted for only 10 months, not 12. After much prayer and meditation, I decided not to apply for renewal. Without funding, we have not been able to operate under the license. We have been paying mortgage, utilities, insurance and maintenance on this building for three years and it no longer makes sense so the building is for sale. It has been a heartbreaking and frustrating experience, and one that points to the undefined and uncoordinated public efforts to deal with addiction.

I've learned to have compassion for the case managers, social workers, doctors, nurses and counselors who work within this dysfunctional system. I know their frustration first hand now, and apologize for my harsh criticism of them. They are limited by bureaucracy. They do not have the time or the freedom to do what is best for the people they serve.

Recently I was contacted by someone who wanted to participate in our program. He had no personal means to pay, but told me he was a client of the state behavioral health system and that he had a wonderful case manager. I told him that we were not a contracted provider but he was determined that he wanted our holistic program. He said he would talk with his case manager and find a way. His case manager came to see me and we shared our frustration. She told me that they do not have adequate services available. The programs that they were contracted with all had waiting lists, and waiting lists do not work well with this population. She also said that we were the only program that she was aware of that offered an alternative to the traditional Twelve Step disease concept model. We agreed that it was important for people to have options; to choose what they felt was best for themselves. It's obvious that adequate services are not available.

Arizona Pathways versus punishment

Punishment becomes the default method of dealing with addiction. Unfortunately, our resources are almost exclusively directed to provide research and social services based on the disease concept model, making it difficult to test the natural theory that I have proposed and tested through using Science of Mind to treat the addict. Society accepts the theory that addiction is a disease, but punishes those experiencing the symptoms. Our prisons are filled with addicts and alcoholics. Probation and parole offices are spending lots of dollars for urine testing, and when they find a client using drugs, he/she is often 'violated' and returned to prison, where he/she is very apt to continue to use drugs. Treatment is unavailable to most of these individuals. Taxpayers pay for prison, parole, urine testing and so forth. But even though we are told these people are suffering from an incurable disease, they are punished, not treated. Treatment based on this theory is based in fear. And in order to stop this cycle, society and effective treatment programs must put into place a way to treat those who started down the path of addictive behaviors because they never had a chance to learn how to be resilient in order to overcome the things in life that lead to addictive behaviors.

Arizona Pathways versus the disease model

Victims of incurable disease must learn to manage and live with it. For the disease of addiction, abstinence is the model, based on support from peers, friends and family. You know what abstinence is if you've ever been on a diet, and you know how often dieters fail to maintain their abstinence. But at least we do not punish dieters and judge them as lesser if they become weak and eat something not allowed on their diet plan. How many people live happy, healthy lives believing they have an incurable disease for which they will be shamed and punished if they allow themselves to experience the symptoms?

What is the divide between people who become sick with cancer, with those who are addicts? One is a disease of the cells; the other is a disease of the spirit. More attention to the role of the human spirit and how it can come to terms with the often harsh hand of life may help get our society to wake up to the

Arizona Pathway's model of treating addictions through Spiritual Principles.

Arizona Pathways versus use of legal drugs

Others believe that if the drug of choice—heroin, alcohol, cocaine, methamphetamines or another drug—is replaced with a synthetic or psychotropic drug or combination of drugs, the victim of the disease of addiction will be relieved of their symptoms and live happily ever after. My experience with clients that are involved with this theory is that they usually add their replacement drug to their drug of choice. They abuse the replacement drugs and often overdose on them, or take them as prescribed and live in an altered state all the time. This also has proven to be extremely expensive and ineffective approach.

We at Arizona Pathways have taken a completely different approach; believing that addiction is a natural outcome for those who do not feel loved, we spend lots of time and effort seeking ways to experience the 'natural high' of experiencing true love. Fortunately, this is inexpensive. At Arizona Pathways, fear of punishment is eliminated and celebration of success is evident. The addict knows that he or she is not less than anyone else, also that they are not victims of an incurable disease. Arizona Pathways teaches that they are the perfect expression of a perfect Creator, and this removes fear and hopelessness. Being accepted, having a chance to learn about their spirit in a gentle way and being able to join a community of others who share their path of growth provides for enthusiasm, courage, health and peace.

Chapter 10:

Ellen Gardner's Life Story

WRITING THIS HAS BEEN A challenging process, starting and stopping for more than ten years. Several people have volunteered to help along the way but somehow for many reasons they quit. I've always used this as an excuse to quit on the project myself. Recently, I experienced a strong desire and intention to finish this project. Again, friends volunteered to help me. In reviewing what I'd written to date, they noticed that something important was missing. So they gave me an assignment: to write my personal story.

I was surprised at my resistance to this request. I was feeling a lot of emotion and hearing myself saying, "I don't want to!" Then I remembered that in my prior attempts to write this book, others who were helping had made similar requests. My response was always that I didn't want to write about me. I wanted to write about Arizona Pathways and the people who are and have been a part of the program. Maybe my helpers from the past quit helping because of my resistance to their suggestions. Maybe I can understand my resistance by completing this writing assignment.

After thinking about it for a while, I realized that people reading this book probably don't know me, and it would be helpful if they knew something about my experiences and personal journey that are the basis for the thoughts, beliefs and ideas that created Arizona Pathways. So I committed to completing this assignment, trusting in its relevance and importance to the whole project. Where do I begin?

At this writing, I am 69 years old; I was born in 1942. That is a lot of years of living and learning. I have witnessed a lot of change in the world, in others and in myself. I was born in a small town on the shores of Lake Michigan, the second of four children. Another sister arrived as number five but I was married and expecting my first son when she was born, so most of my family experiences didn't include her. Neither parent had more than an 8th grade education. My mother was the eldest of four children who grew up during the Depression. Her father was the town drunk. She was 15 when she married my father. He was 21. My dad was the second of seven children. His mother was a fanatical Southern Baptist. His family moved to Michigan from Tennessee when he was still a kid. His father worked in a factory. My dad also was a factory worker.

When I was about 2 years old, my dad was drafted to fight in World War II. He was very resentful of being drafted because he was one day short of the cut off age of 26, and he was married with two children. Of course I don't remember those times and only have memories of what I was told. I know that even as a toddler, I didn't feel like I was in the right family. My mother tells stories of how I would disappear as a toddler and she would either find me at Mrs. Ingalls, taking a bath in her kitchen sink, or at the neighbor's house on the other side eating chocolate chip cookies. As a mother myself, I can't imagine how that could happen!

When daddy came home from the army, we moved to an old farmhouse in the country. By this time, I had a baby sister. I loved the country and became my daddy's shadow. Wherever he went, I was with him. I know that I was daddy's girl and somehow I felt my older sister was mommy's girl. My dad used to tell me that I had a "mean" mama and I believed him. I never bonded with her and felt that she didn't love me and that my sister was the important and loved one. I reflect on why I felt this way and think that my mom felt treated so unfairly as the eldest child in her family that she was determined not to let her eldest have a similar experience. I think because of this, she overcompensated for her part in the treatment of her own children. I'm sure she was unaware of the danger of abuse by allowing me to belong to my dad.

I blocked out a lot of awareness of what happened in those early childhood years. The only affection I remembered was from my dad. He took care of me when I was sick. He taught me how to ride a bike, how to fish, how to work in the garden and how to care for the animals. My parents did not have a happy marriage. There was a lot of fighting, yelling and name-calling. When I was 5, I had a baby brother. We were all thrilled with him. Gradually, as he grew enough to do things with daddy, I found myself feeling left out often. I was in school, had friends and was basically happy. My friends filled the gap along with Cindy, my cocker spaniel. I never cried, no matter what, until I could go out in the woods with Cindy. I told her everything that hurt, angered or scared me and sometimes I would cry and she would comfort me.

I experienced puberty very young. It was the summer before 5th grade, so I was going on 10 when I got my first period. My mother never had "that" talk with me. I know she and my older sister had some "private" talks and my sister had a booklet from the Kotex company that I was not supposed to see. When I woke up that morning, bleeding, I thought I had hurt myself or something. I told mom I was bleeding and she just said, "The stuff you need is in the bathroom closet." She then left, taking my older sister with her. I felt scared and abandoned. I was also responsible to take care of my little sister and brother. Thankfully, one of our friends, who was 12 or 13, stopped over and she explained to me what was going on and that I was okay. She said it was a good thing and I should be proud to be grown up so fast. My dad changed how he treated me and it felt like he didn't want me anymore. Now I was nobody's little girl. I spent a lot of time talking about it with my loyal dog, Cindy.

Things stayed the same for about two years. I loved school, had good friends. I always worked to earn money. I picked berries all summer and babysat a lot. I convinced myself that I didn't need anybody and did my best to be independent. The summer before 8th grade, we moved back to town. My mom and my older sister hated the country and our old farmhouse. My dad and I wanted to stay in the country, but we moved to town anyway.

For 8th grade in the city I went to school at a junior high school. Gone was the 3 grades per room country schoolhouse. Gone were old friends, the farmhouse and the comfort of my safe place with Cindy out in the woods. My older sister was happy because her boyfriend lived here. My mom was happy, her job was here and she hated the old farmhouse. My little brother and sister didn't seem to care one way or another. Dad was miserable and so was I.

In town there were rich kids, poor kids and some in between. It seemed like if you didn't have the best clothes, and didn't live in the right neighborhood, you weren't good enough. I remember being invited to go home with a friendly girl from the rich group. The first questions her parents asked me were "Where does your father work?" followed by "Where do you live?" Needless to say they didn't approve of my answers. Their daughter was always friendly and nice to me at school, but I was never invited to go home with her again.

I did well in school and made friends. I met my first boyfriend. I was 13 and he was a senior football player. He was nice and treated me well. He was the first of many older boyfriends. I didn't think about it then, but now I look back and notice that when my dad began to either ignore me or beat me, I found "older" boys to fill the void. My sister and I used to go to Sunday school when we lived in the country. When we moved to town, I went to the Baptist church that my dad's family attended. They had a wonderful young peoples' group and a young inspiring minister. I later left my football player for a church boyfriend. He too was older.

These were difficult times for me. I didn't feel accepted by the popular students or my own family. About this time I developed a habit of embellishing the stories of my experiences. I was always attempting to find acceptance by my parents and sisters. I would do everything I could to please them or I would decide that I didn't need them and I didn't care if they loved me or not. I always worked to earn money for what I needed or wanted. I picked berries, babysat, cleaned houses and worked at the beach concessions. I stayed away from home as much as I could.

When I was 14, and in 9th grade, I met my first real love. He was 19. My mom never talked to me about boys, sex, dating or anything personal. Most of our conversations were about chores and curfews. About this same time, my best friend Joyce did a wonderful thing for me. She confronted me on all the "whoppers" I was telling. She told me that she loved me and wanted me to know that no one believed my stories anyway. She agreed to help me break the habit by reminding me when I started telling tales. I'll always be thankful for her help.

One Sunday, one of my friends from church wanted to come home with me for a few hours after church. She lived quite far away and wanted to stay in town to go to a special program at church that evening. I had told her about my father's "black" moods and his violence toward me when one of those moods hit him. This particular Sunday afternoon, it happened while she was there. My dad just opened my bedroom door, grabbed me and started hitting and calling me names. She was scared when I returned to the room. She said she didn't believe me when I told her that this often happened. I understood then that because I embellished and made up so much, people didn't believe me. I decided that day to always tell the truth.

My boyfriend met my family. He was always polite and made sure I was home by curfew. I really believed we were in love and that he was the most important person in the world. I guess my mom got worried about how serious we seemed to be although she never talked to me about it. Behind my back she arranged for the people I babysat for to make sure that I got home much later than usual. When my 19-year old boyfriend came to pick me up, I wasn't home yet. My mother told him that he had to stay away from me. I was too young for him. She threatened to go to the police if he ever called me or saw me again.

When I got home I knew I was late for our date. I asked if he had been there or called. My mother said "no." I was devastated! A few days later my girlfriend who was dating the brother of my boyfriend told me what had happened. I remember the anger and hurt was overwhelming. I stayed in my room almost all the time. The police had stopped my boyfriend several times, warning him to stay away from me. Small town cops! School was out a couple of months later. I was so depressed.

One day I looked in the medicine cabinet and my eyes focused on a bottle that said "for external use only." I opened the bottle and drank the stuff. I went to my room and tried to go to sleep. I was suddenly very sick. My mom heard me and came in and discovered the empty bottle. My dad was at work, so she called my uncle and he came and took me to the hospital. There they pumped my stomach and kept me for a couple of days.

I was 14, no one asked me what was wrong. It all just confirmed my belief that I didn't matter. When I was released nothing was said. A couple of my church friends called but said nothing about the incident. The sad thing about it was that it all seemed pretty normal at the time. A couple of months later my aunt and uncle from Arizona came for a visit. I always really loved Aunt Lauretta. They said I could go back to Arizona with them and go to school there. Amazingly, my parents agreed to let me go. Of course there was no discussion with me but I didn't care. I was excited to experience this adventure and to be with people who actually wanted me.

I made friends easily and did well in school. No one asked me what my father did or why I was living with my aunt and uncle. They just accepted me. I was happy for a change. My aunt and uncle both worked and they had two little boys. I did a lot of babysitting and housecleaning for them. I didn't want to be a problem. I didn't want to go back to Michigan. Of course after a few months, I started dating an older man. He was 26, I was 15. He was a good person and I was happy with him. I probably would have outgrown him in time but my parents insisted I return to Michigan after the school year ended. I didn't want to go back but they came to get me. Why did they insist that I return to live with them when they really didn't seem to like me? I had to leave a place when I felt accepted, loved and safe.

Within a few days, my father started the unprovoked violent attacks. I overheard my two sisters saying, "Why did she have to come back here?" That was the unanswered question. This was all happening in the mid 1950's. This was a time of secrets, gossip and hypocrisy. If no one talked about what happened, it was as if nothing happened. This was a time when the adults were always telling the truth and the teenagers were always told that they were lying. Shortly after my return "home" I was babysitting for a state policeman and his wife's children. When the parents came home, the husband (a state police officer) was taking me home. He attempted to kiss me and touch me inappropriately. I pushed him away and told him to let me out of the car. I walked the rest of the way home. I didn't say anything about what he did.

A few days later, I was summoned to the Juvenile Court. This man filed a complaint about me claiming that I entertained men who were drinking alcohol in his home when I was supposed to be caring for his children. Of course I denied the charges because this wasn't the truth. I wasn't believed, he was. I was placed on unofficial probation for six months. This was just one of many experiences that validated my lack of trust in authority.

When school started that fall, I was beginning the 11th grade. Things were not going well. I was talking to my Arizona boyfriend weekly and really wanting to return to Arizona. He encouraged me to be patient and do my best to get along until I was old enough to leave or until could convince my parents to agree. I made up my mind to do my best. Once school started, I became aware that I was being shunned by many who had previously been friendly. I attempted to join in activities offered but was rejected. Finally one of my friends told me that her parents told her not to associate with me because they had heard that I had gone to Arizona last year to have a baby. This was not true, but at this time if a teenage girl went away to live with her aunt the only believable reason was to have a baby. At last now I understood why I was being rejected.

School was stressful and I was miserable. My boyfriend from Arizona asked my mother if he could come to get me. Would she sign permission for me to marry him? I was 16, he was 27. Surprisingly she said "yes." Good, I could go back to a place where I had been happy. I told my boyfriend that it was important to me to graduate from high school. He agreed. I was planning on continuing my education once I was back in Arizona. There was no additional conversation regarding my getting married and returning to Arizona.

I expected my Knight in Shining Armor to arrive any day. About five days went by when one of my friends told me that they had seen a car that fit the description I had shared with Arizona license plates being stopped by the State Police just outside of the city limits. I heard nothing from my boyfriend, no phone calls, no letters. Again, I was abandoned by someone I trusted, someone I loved. It never dawned on me at the time that my mother had done it again. She had the police watch and turn him back. She never had any intention of signing permission for us to be married. I was underage and he was threatened with arrest. My self-esteem was so low that I didn't even suspect what had happened. She told him that he was not to contact me at all. I experienced abandonment and rejection. I refused to continue attending the local high school and asked to go live with my grandmother and go to school in her town. My parents refused to let me go so I just quit. I found work cleaning houses, babysitting, picking berries, washing dishes and working at the beach. I bought a car. Finally my grandmother and I convinced my parents that I could live with her and I promised to go to school. I had earned extra credit earlier so I was permitted to start the new school as a senior even though I had dropped out of in the first semester of the 11th grade.

Again I felt accepted and happy. Many of the students were from the country school I had attended years ago. They remembered me and welcomed me. My grandmother worked as a telephone operator and she helped me to get a part time job at the telephone office. I graduated on time with good grades.

Shortly after graduation my older sister, who was married and living in married housing at Michigan State University had some serious medical problems. When she was released from the hospital she needed help at home. I was happy to go help for a week or so. While I was there her husband who was a student took me on a guided tour of the campus. During our tour I picked up an application for admission, just out of curiosity. My brother in law laughed at me and told me that I would never be accepted to the University. Well, I also responded strongly to reverse psychology. I filled out and submitted the application. Wow miracles do happen! I was accepted! My parents were surprised. We had never talked about college. I had some money saved and my mom was working and said she could help. My sister and her husband said I could live with them which would make at least the first year affordable. Unfortunately when I arrived and checked in to register for school I was informed that the rules were that freshmen had to live in the dormitory unless they lived at home. They were not willing to accept that living with my sister qualified as living at home. So the cost of college suddenly doubled. Well, I tried to make the best of things hoping I could find a job to help with the costs. I made it through two semesters and ran out of money.

I returned home and soon became engaged to the guy I had been dating in high school He was only one year older than me which was different. We were the best of friends. We both were employed and were saving for our life together. I grew close to his family and loved them very much. They were the model for our marriage.

When we got married my husband was 21. I was still 19. Things were good until our son was born. I found myself alone with a baby while my husband went out. He was older, old enough to drink. I wasn't He started drinking a lot and often became violent. It was like living at home with my father all over again. I left him many times and he would promise me that he would quit drinking and that he wouldn't hurt me. He kept breaking his the promises. I filed for divorce but let our minister talk me out of it. My husband was drinking, seeing other women, and always losing jobs.

When my son was six months old, I had to have minor surgery to deal with problems relating to childbirth. I went back to work right away because we needed the money. I came home from work, picked up my son at the baby sitter and couldn't wait to go to bed early and rest. I was exhausted. I thought my husband was at work. He was working the second shift at the local tannery. I had just put the baby to bed, taken a bath and put my pajamas on when my best friend Joyce showed up. She was upset. Someone told her that they had seen our husbands out drinking together instead of being at work. She wanted to go find them. I told her no, I was tired and ready for bed. Finally she convinced me that her mother in law would take care of my son and she and I should at least just go out for pizza or something. We took my baby to her mother in law. She also had two children who were there.

As we were heading for the pizza place we came across the husbands. Her husband was driving and my husband ducked down. Joyce was sure that there was a girl in the car and that was she who ducked down. I told her that I was pretty sure that it was my husband. She convinced me to follow them. It appeared they were headed to the house. They were going fast.

Suddenly they took an unexpected curve. I followed and lost control of the car. It rolled and rolled. It seemed like the loud crashing was going on forever. Joyce had been thrown out on the first roll I was thrown out closer to where the car stopped. I started looking for Joyce, calling her name. Then I noticed that my body was still lying on the ground motionless near the car. Yet I knew I was looking for her.

Our husbands had seen my headlights up in the sky so they knew we had crashed. They came back to the scene, then ran to a house to ask for them to call for help. I told them I couldn't find Joyce. They said they found her and she was hurt. I couldn't move. I was very cold. The ambulance came and picked us up. Joyce's husband Gary rode in the back of the ambulance. I asked him how she was. He said he didn't know but she had a big cut on her head. She was unconscious. My husband drove Gary's car and followed the ambulance. Two drunken men were suddenly very sober.

Because this was a small town there wasn't a doctor at the hospital. One had to be called in. The nurses on duty were upset because they determined that Joyce needed a transfusion and they were required to wait for a doctor. I suddenly became aware that I could see and hear everything that was happening in the emergency room. I could see me lying on a table, I could see Joyce on another table. Our husbands were pacing, calling family and hitting the walls. Then I heard Joyce talking to me and I realized that we both were up near the ceiling. We could see and hear each other but no one could see or hear us.

Joyce told me that she didn't want to return to her body lying below us. She said she was ready to move on. She said to me, "Come on, come with me!" I tried to convince her to stay. I talked about her two small children, her parents, and her sister. I promised I would help her if she wanted to divorce her husband. I promised I would work and help support her and the kids. She continued to attempt to persuade me to go with her. It was her persistent persuasion that got me to leave home that night, her strong persuasion that encouraged me to follow our husbands that night. I reminded her that this whole incident was her idea. She agreed but she insisted that she was leaving. She told me that she had already made her mother promise to be sure her children were well cared for and that they were told about their mother and how much she loved them.

Joyce reminded me that my marriage was miserable, my husband was violent, that he was a drunk and a womanizer just like her husband. I heard everything she said and she was right.

Maybe, leaving these bodies behind was a good idea. We began to notice a glowing light, like a sunrise getting larger and closer. Joyce said "see, it's beautiful, feel it, it feels free and happy."

"Yes" I said, "I see it and feel it. It feels wonderful. It feels like it is calling us or pulling us, doesn't it?"

Joyce said, "Yes, and look I am not fat anymore." (Joyce's father was Hawaiian and she was beautiful but always large in size. She gained a lot of weight bringing two children into the world. She always thought her fat was why her husband drank and cheated on her with other women.) I looked at her and smiled.

I said, "You are so beautiful and you are right, you are not fat anymore." She was smiling and tried one last time to persuade me to come with her. When I told her that I really felt that I had to stay she asked me if I would stay in touch with her mother and her children. Then she said, "Look—there is my grandmother, she is here to meet me." Joyce never regained consciousness.

The hospital staff told me that I kept going in and out of consciousness. Several times they thought I was not going to make it. Well, obviously I did. My injuries were extensive, concussion, broken collarbone, breastbone, several ribs, several pelvic fractures, and several smashed vertebrae that were all jammed together. I was in shock yet I knew Joyce was dead. I felt so sad and so responsible. It was a couple of days before I was told the extent of my injuries. The doctor came in to tell me when my husband and parents were there. He said he had talked to an orthopedic specialist and I would need surgery. Then he told me that I may become paralyzed, there was not guarantee that they could fix my back.

For some reason, I had a strong conviction that surgery was not the right thing for me. I just knew this and I refused to agree to the operation. The doctor said he would talk to more specialists because this was way out of his expertise. The next day he returned to tell me that another doctor reviewed the x-rays and suggested trying traction. His idea was based on the belief that our bodies heal themselves but often needed assistance. He designed traction that would take all the weight and pressure off the broken bones. So they turned the bed around and arched my back over where people usually supported their knees.

So my head was hanging down and my back was arched in a backbend. This was to create space without weight or pressure to allow the broken vertebrae to spread apart and grow back together on their own.

Next a sling was placed under my butt to take the pressure off my broken pelvis and a lot of weight was secured to my feet. The doctor said this may or may not work but if it didn't, maybe I would be open to surgery.

Here I was strung up for a month, not able to do anything for myself. I hung there and looked out the window. It snowed everyday. People came to visit. The minister came every day. My husband came often but not nearly as often as I needed him to. My mother came every day to feed me. I told her she didn't have to come out in the bad weather. I still don't know why she did it; we weren't close. We didn't talk. I didn't remember her ever taking care of me. When I was little it was always my daddy. He didn't come much. My grandmother sent me a card everyday. Everyone at the hospital was wonderful!

My mother and my husband went to Joyce's funeral. They came to see me afterward. My mother said, "Joyce really looked beautiful and peaceful and you know what? She didn't look fat at all."

I said, "I know." I didn't tell anyone about the shared out of body time that Joyce and I had. Sometimes I thought I imagined it, that maybe it was just part of the shock. But when my mother talked about how she looked at the funeral, I knew it was true. I cried a lot. I felt guilty and responsible for the accident and for Joyce's death. Her parents came to see me. They were so sad!

They said that they didn't blame me and that they were glad that I survived.

Joyce's mother told me that she knew something like this was going to happen. She said that Joyce had made her promise to look after her children. She also told me that Joyce had picked out a tombstone about a month ago. About two months before that, Joyce had a rollover accident with her mother's car. That time no one was seriously injured.

The police also came to talk with me. They asked if I was on medication. They asked about the car. My husband had bought it about a week prior to the accident. I was angry about it because we couldn't afford it. In my anger I told him if he didn't take it back I would wreck it. I really didn't plan on doing that. The police told me that based on the inspection it appeared that the brakes were faulty and that this probably contributed to the accident. I told them that it might be true but I admitted to driving too fast and that I should not have followed our husbands. They did not issue any citations. I think I wanted them to punish me for causing my best friend to die.

This was a very difficult time. I missed my 6-month-old baby. I worried about my job, my home, my marriage. I worried about everything because I could do nothing. I had always convinced myself that I didn't need anybody. This was really hard!

The whole month of December I hung there in traction watching the snowfall, crying, praying, feeling guilty. I was taking a lot of painkillers and told them I thought I was healed enough to get out of the traction after two weeks, so they took the weights off. I changed my mind quickly—the pain was overwhelming. When I was actually in the traction the pain was minimal. After 30 days it was much better. The x-rays were positive—the broken bones had moved back in place perfectly.

So they sent me home to my parents with a hospital bed, a bedpan, crutches and a wheelchair. I still had to sleep with m head down and my back arched but I could sit up and feed myself. My brother was 15 at the time. He was so kind and helpful. He would lift me up and carry me to the bathroom before he went to school and come home for lunch to do the same. He knew I didn't want to use the bedpan and I wasn't very good with the crutches.

After I was doing quite well he took me ice fishing. He carried me to the car, then when we got to the lake he pulled me down to the ice on a sled. It was my first outing since the accident and it was wonderful.

My husband was trying hard to be supportive and he came over with my baby often. Times sure have changed. There was no physical therapy or counseling. No one talked about the accident or asked how I felt about it. I didn't talk about it either. I wore an elastic brace on my back several moths. I didn't take pain pills after I left the hospital. Sixty days after the accident, I went home to my own house with my husband and my son. Thirty days later I was back to work. Things were okay for a while.

Then my husband lost his job and couldn't find another one. We moved about 40 miles away to a larger city. Both of us found work right away. Soon the old behavior was back. My husband drinking, not going to work, leaving me at work without a way home, yet beating me for having one of the boys from work bring me home. It was an impossible situation.

One night he came home drunk and started hitting me and I found myself up near the ceiling watching. This was familiar. I remembered doing this in the emergency room with Joyce and I had a strong feeling that I had left myself often when I was a little girl.

This time I promised God that if I didn't die that night that I would leave this marriage, never to return. My husband left to go deer hunting for a week with his father. While he was gone I went to a lawyer and filed for a divorce. When he came home, I stayed with friends until he was served with the divorce papers and an order of protection. When I thought I was safe I returned home with my son. My husband was gone and so were all his clothes and personal stuff. A friend came with her son to stay with me for a few months. The idea was that she would stay with the children while I went to work.

A few days later while we were watching TV after the kids were in bed, a brick came crashing through the window. Then I heard someone kick in the back door then I heard footsteps coming up the stairs. I told my friend to leave and go up to the landlady's apartment to call the police. I knew it was my husband. He came in swinging and throwing things. I was sure this was the end of me. The police finally showed up and made him leave but they wouldn't take him into custody.

About half an hour later the phone rang. It was my husband. He told me to come pick him up. I told him no. Then he said, "I'll be right there." I called the police to report the call and his threat to return to my apartment. The police told me to call them if he showed up. I knew that there would be no time to call them when he showed up so I took the kids and my friend and left. I had to quit my job because of the bruises and burns on my face. Even though my parents were far from the perfect parents, I knew I could go "home" for help. That night I vowed that no one was ever going to hit me ever again. I was 21. Now, more than 40 years later—no one has hit me and I believe no one will.

As soon as the bruises and marks were healed I found a job. My plan was to save some money and find a safe place for my son and myself. My son's father would come often to see his son. He would always tell me that he was changing and that he wasn't drinking. He'd remind me of the good times, of how we were best friends and how much he loved me and our son. I still felt the tug on my heart but I remembered my promise to leave the marriage. I knew I could never trust him not to hurt me or our son. He refused to pay the child support that the court ordered him to pay. After being arrested for not paying it he went to Texas because he knew that Texas would not cooperate with the other states to enforce child support. At least I finally felt safe.

I was almost ready to move from my parents to my own place when my mother announced that she was divorcing my father. They had been married for 27 years.

They had always been miserable so I was surprised that they were divorcing after all this time. My little sister was about three and my brother was about sixteen. My father blamed me. He thought I had convinced my mom to file for the divorce. My mother told me that she needed me to stay to help support her, my sister and brother. She convinced me that I would be very selfish to move out when she needed help. She was working nights and I worked days so we could take care of the kids without needing a babysitter. So for about two years we lived together. My mother also took in other single moms to help pay the bills. This was a very unhealthy and unhappy environment.

I dated some but I was very untrusting of relationships. Older men were interesting and I dated a couple. At least I thought that they could provide security. I soon understood that if I was willing to depend on them that I would have to give up my independence. No way was I willing to be a possession!

I had been working about 35 miles from home. My boss offered to loan me a down payment on a small house close to work. I accepted and finally moved out of the craziness. I was dating my current husband when I moved. A few months later we got married. He has two children by his previous marriage. About six months after we were married his ex-wife asked us to take his kids for a while because she was having problems. They were 5 and 7. So for a year we had three kids. For the most part it was fun and it was sad when their mother came and took them back. They moved to another state so we only saw them for summer. There was always a feeling of uncertainty about if they would come live with us again. One of the things we would do when we had all three kids was to take a ride out in the country on Sunday afternoons. I still missed the old farmhouse of my childhood and I had always wanted a horse, particularly a black one.

One Sunday afternoon we found an old farmhouse for sale. It was only about ¼ mile down the road from my aunt Margie's. We put our house up for sale and it sold quickly. We bought the old farmhouse which was on 10 acres. It needed a lot of work but we loved it. It had a barn so we bought a couple of horses. My husband worked hard to remodel the house and barn. My father came over a lot to help. He loved to drive the tractor so he was always there to cut and bale hay and help with the huge garden. The love of the country and the old farmhouses was still something my dad and I had in common. We lived here when my younger son was born. Now sometimes we had two kids, sometimes four or five. My mom and dad both would come over and bring my little sister.

I always cooked a lot of food on the weekends because we always had a lot of people to feed. Life was good on the farm. I even finally had a black Arabian stallion. He was the most beautiful horse I had ever seen. My husband and I worked together to show him in horse shows and to promote him for breeding. We soon had baby horses and lots of work.

We also went into a business partnership with my boss. So my husband ran the manufacturing factory and I was responsible for the office part. We worked hard, learned a lot and made a comfortable living.

I had always suffered with severe headaches. When I was only 8-10 years old I had migraines. Then they would almost disappear only to return later. When life seemed almost perfect they returned with a vengeance. At least once a week I would find myself violently ill with these headaches. Often I ended up needing a shot of Demerol for relief. Finally the doctor said he didn't know how to help but he said drugs were not a good solution. He suggested that we try another climate.

Well, I had always wanted to return to Arizona. My husband wasn't so sure but he agreed to take a trip to explore the west. He thought Colorado or New Mexico might be interesting. So he and I took a vacation to explore. Flagstaff, in Arizona, appealed to both of us. It is beautiful country.

We found a retail store for sale and were able to get a Small Business Administration loan to buy it. So back to Michigan to sell our farm. It sold in a week! We headed to Arizona with two boys, two horses and limited personal stuff to arrive on July 4, 1973.

We built a new house and learned how to run a retail business. For the most part we enjoyed life. Flagstaff was friendly. The climate was easy to adapt to from what we were used to in Michigan. Arizona has a lot more sun and we liked that.

We had some difficult financial times and had to sell the horses and move into town. I had to find a job and my husband ran the store. The developers started building shopping malls and the big chain stores were coming in. The local "mom and pop" businesses were disappearing.

I went back to college and decided to pursue an accounting degree. For some reason I had always found jobs in the accounting area. Then the company I was working for merged with a larger company and moved me to Phoenix. Our store was no longer profitable so we liquidated it. Again our house sold quickly and in 1981 we moved to the Valley, to Chandler, Arizona.

My husband found a good job quickly. I transferred from Northern Arizona University in Flagstaff to Arizona State University in Tempe and worked full time at the new company. My oldest son was eighteen and he chose to stay in Flagstaff.

It didn't take long to become aware that I was uncomfortable in the new company. It was a real "good ol' boys" club. I was the chief accountant of the Arizona division so I could see that the president and his cronies were taking huge salaries and doing little or no work. At first I told myself just to do a good job, pray about it and believe I could be a positive influence to the whole. As it came time for final exams at the end of the semester, the president told me to take some time off to finish up the semester. At first I thought he was being kind and helpful. But then he said that I would be assigned another position when I returned. He said he had hired a CPA and I would work under him. I decided that this just wasn't the best place for me so I resigned. Later I learned that the company soon was dissolved and several of the "good ol' boys" were in prison on fraud charges.

As soon as my final exams were over I looked for a new job. I applied at an agency that specialized in accounting positions. The agency owner offered me a position finding jobs for accountants. This was new and interesting so I decided to give it a try. I found that I was quite good at it and was earning more money than I ever had before. The agency owner was a tyrant and very hard to work with but I did my best to please her and get along. One day when I came into work she told me that she was letting me go. She gave no reason other than to say that it wasn't working out. At that time she owed me several thousand dollars in commissions. I asked her if she was going to pay me what I had earned and if she would release me from the non-compete agreement I had signed when she hired me. She said no to both questions. I hired a lawyer and she did have to pay me, but I was not released from the non-compete agreement.

I tried several things after that. I worked for New York Life Insurance Company as an insurance agent, then for Waddell and Reed as a financial planner and a few other sales jobs. I went to school and got a real estate license and worked in business brokerage for a while.

Finally I realized that I needed to understand what was causing me to connect with people who seemed to treat me unfairly. I prayed about it and decided that I would only work in an honest, harmonious and supportive environment. Things changed. The non-compete time had elapsed and I was hired as an executive recruiter for the nicest people I had ever worked with.

Some time later I had an opportunity to purchase the agency that had fired me years before. The owner that I had worked for had sold the agency and the newcomers were not doing well. They sold it to me at a very reasonable price and terms. Now I had my own business again and things went very well for a few years.

During this time I was introduced to Religious Science and took all the classes that they offered. After completing this training I then went to seminary at the Living Bible Center and became an ordained minister. This all led to the beginning of my work with the addicted population.

A recession hit and I closed my employment agency and continued to work with the addicted. I began a small church that evolved into what is now Arizona Pathways of Live, Unity and Love.

In remembering my life story I became aware of how much I have changed over the years. Just like most people, I formed beliefs about myself and the world as I experienced life. As a child I probably thought that the world was about me so I took everything and everyone personally. Then I developed expectations based on this limited, erroneous perception. Some of these expectations were: that my parents were qualified to meet my idea of perfect parents; the world must be fair; I would be loved by everyone unconditionally especially my parents; I would always be treated equally with my siblings and everyone else; I was always safe and protected. Obviously, most of my expectations were unmet.

My responses and new beliefs became: I am unloved, unlovable and often hated; life was unfair; I am not important, worthy, believed, safe or protected. I became convinced that I was deserving of abuse. Through the years I kept trying to find a way to get my family to love me. When it seemed useless I would be determined not to need them to love me, not to care, not to depend on anyone for anything. Obviously, I found ways to survive. Some of my survival tools were: denial; creating fantasies and making up stories about a different environment; escape by running away from home, or working and finding opportunities to live with other people; isolating, developing independence; stuffing feelings and refusing to react to them; and when things were really traumatic, I could just dissociate and hang out near the ceiling.

I have had a strong faith in God as far back as I can remember. Often I was the only one in the family to attend church. Sometimes I didn't go either, but I always prayed and believed God heard me. As I became a young adult or maybe still a teenager I knew that surviving was not enough. I was sure God wanted me to thrive!

I began exploring different religions and philosophies. Always an avid reader, I read about all kinds of cultures, lifestyles, religions, etc. As I pursued more understanding and spiritual awareness I was drawn to the tools that would help me to move past surviving to thriving. I learned to not only pray but to meditate, to listen for guidance and direction. I found I needed to learn to communicate honestly and openly without expectations of others. Forgiveness lessons became obvious and continuous. I began to make friends who were kind, honest and unconditionally loving. Every day my faith became stronger.

The scripture from Romans 12:2 reminded me of what I must do, "And be not conformed to this world: be ye transformed by the renewing of your mind, that ye may prove what is the good and acceptable, and perfect will of God." It was plain to me that my mind was filled with mistaken ideas and beliefs and if I wanted to experience God's will I needed to change my mind about all the lack and limitations and blame and resentment.

Like it is written in Proverbs 23.7, "For as a man thinketh in his heart, so is he." I wasn't happy with who I had thought I was, so of course I wasn't happy with my life experience. I recognized that I had been living a false identity.

Romans 8.16, "The spirit itself beareth witness with our Sprit, that we are the children of God" and I John 4.4, "Ye are of God, little children, and have overcome them because greater is he that is in you than he that is in the world." There is no possibility that I could ever be less than a child of God and be like God. All my doubts, fear, insecurity, resentful feelings and beliefs in lack and limitations stem from the illusion that I could be anything less than what God created me to be.

Another scripture, Acts 17: 27-28 says, "That they should seek the Lord, if haply they might feel after him, and find him though he be not far from everyone of us, for in him we live, and move and have our being, as certain also of your own poets have said, for we are his offspring."

There are many additional references to our true identity as spiritual children of God.

Forgiving mother

Forgiveness is lifetime work. As I was learning to understand myself as a child of God, I became very aware of feelings of resentment I still had for my mother. She used to come to Arizona to spend the winter months with us every year. These were difficult times for me because all the old feelings would come up. One day I was sharing this with a close friend and she suggested that I write what I was feeling. So here is what I wrote:

Ellen Gardner, L.I.S.A.C.

My Perfect Mother

12/25/89

What is a perfect mother?
I always thought it was someone
that didn't favor one child over another.
It was someone who was kind and loving,
someone who talked with me and explained how life works,
someone who cooked and cleaned and healed my hurts,
someone who made me feel confident, loved and secure,
someone who for all of my problems had the cure.
A perfect mother was also a perfect wife,
pleasing Daddy and making things nice.
A perfect mother gives guidance and encouragement,
to fulfill all your dreams.
A perfect mother loves unconditionally, never judging,
never condemning, or blaming,
never using harsh words, never being mean.
Growing up, my mother certainly didn't seem to fit this
mold. She usually seemed sad, angry, hateful and cold. I
understand now that she couldn't give what she didn't have.
All those things I needed from her, she needed too.
But I now know, my mother is the perfect mother for me,
without her being just as she is,
I wouldn't be me!
To fulfill my dreams and follow my heart,
A dysfunctional family was the perfect start.
It was through her sadness and suffering, I've learned to care.
Through trail and tribulation, I've learned compassion
and how to share.
Books and teachers have given me knowledge,
but experience gave me understanding.
My mother was the perfect mother for me, I see that clearly

now, as I've learned to set myself free, from anger, fear,
guilt and blame, no longer bound by unearned shame.
I no longer live by the need to be right,
I understand how all things work together for our good
There is no enemy, nothing to fight.
So thank you mom, for your love and caring
Though previously lost in our pain and suffering,
Through understanding the past,
there is forgiveness and sharing.
Your are the perfect mom for me.
It's our lessons shared that have given to me
the tools of my trade, to do Our Creator's will,
Unconditional love, forgiveness, compassion
and understanding.
I love you just the way you are!
Thanks for being my mom!

I did feel better after writing it. At my friend's suggestion,
I had it printed on pretty paper and framed it and gave it to my
mother for Christmas. I was afraid she might be hurt or angry
but she wasn't! She gave me the first hug I could ever remember.
We will never be close like I thought I wanted to be, but the
resentment is gone and we accept each other just as we are today.
The past is gone, but it did influence who we are now.

Many of the clients of Arizona Pathways have similar mother
or father issues. Some have thanked me for sharing this writing
with them. Along my spiritual journey, I do a lot of writing and
encourage our clients to do the same. Often I will spend time in
meditation and then pick up a pen and write. Following are some
my writings.

Being a warrior

In the silence, I hear it, the encouragement, the inspiration, the promise. I am a warrior but not a war. My battle is within. I must release the beliefs that are blocks and trust in the truth that comforts. I do not fight. But I stand on the truth, fearless. It matters not what others do, or think, or say. My truth is strong and solid. As I stay firm in my trust, I am strong and solid. I will never move. The solid place is within, where I had thought the battle was. There is no battle, no war. It was only an illusion. The fog of my human mind clouded my vision. But I see clearly now. God is Love. I am Love. Love is the answer to all human concerns. The light of Love pierces and removes the fog and the illusion gives way to the beauty of oneness. I am powerful in my ego powerlessness. I trust in the Oneness. My day is now. Now is any moment in time that I am aware of the unity of Life and my important expression of this unity, my part, your part is unique, individual, yet one and the same.

In the darkness and stillness of human experience the light of truth still shines from within. I must be still to experience the light. My human mind speaks of the darkness even while knowing that the light is still there. It is while in the darkness that I experience the light, the light of truth, the light of awareness. This light comforts me in times of dark experiences. I live in the light. I am the light. In the silence the darkness matters not. The darkness passes. The light is always present. I let the darkness come and pass on. It brings lessons. It sometimes causes pain. But it reminds me of the light that is within me, the light that I am. Sometimes from the place of light within I can see others experiencing the darkness. I offer my light to guide them to their own inner light. Sometimes they are joyful and accept. Sometimes they choose to remain in the darkness. This is not bad or wrong or sad. It is just a choice of what to experience.

The light is always there!

Words of inspiration from the Father within

The fullest expression of my good is yours. There is truly no loss, lack or limitation. Opportunities are abundant. The door is open and I am guiding you through.

You must remember never to accept as truth someone else's perception of you. You do know yourself. You are very sure of what you believe and what you feel. You do know what to do and what to say at all times in all situations, because it is I who expresses through you. Do not listen to your ego, which feels attacked and wounded by the opinions of others. In our work, you will often serve as a mirror to others. This does not mean that what they see is a part of you. Just as a reflection in the water is not part of the water, it is only an image cast upon it. Do not be confused. In order to stay perfectly clear, it is important for you to remember that you are my perfect offspring. It is only your ego that reacts to the outer feelings and it is your ego that accepts the judgments and causes anger and resentment to enter your consciousness. Be aware of your tendency to judge and criticize others, for you are only seeing in them a part of your ego-self as a reflection in them. Resist anger and resentment, do not judge, love only. Accept everyone as your brother or sister and love him or her as you love me. Accept yourself as my child, my friend and my partner. There truly is no separation. As you hold to this truth, you will be free from all negativity. Trust me, for I love you dearly. I have created you to express me in a special way. The way to be that perfect expression is to listen and hear your hearts desire and to follow your heart!

I continue to do my best to follow this guidance. I encourage everyone to follow their heart no matter where it takes them, but to be sure of their commitment because there is no turning back. This is the narrow path mentioned in the Bible, that we are called to travel. It is too narrow to turn around in. If you attempt to turn around, you will just get stuck until you become willing to continue forward.

I've learned that God's way is often mysterious. The form our life takes when we "let" God create and express through us is often quite different from what we think it should be. I never imagined my "church" would be related to addiction. God created it and maintains it that way. What I realize is that I am required to give up my attachment to how I think things should be.

God knows best!

==THE END==

About the Author

Photo by Whitney Billings

Ellen Gardner witnessed addiction in loved ones. Motivated to help, she learned to see them as teachers. Arizona Pathways of Life, Unity and Love Residential Program in Phoenix, AZ is her calling—a holistic, spiritually based solution. Ellen is married to Daniel and has two adult children.

CPSIA information can be obtained at www.ICGtesting.com
Printed in the USA
BVOW011338201112

306041BV00001B/61/P